ACROSS
THE
BORDER

ACROSS THE BORDER

THE TRUE STORY OF THE SATANIC CULT KILLINGS IN MATAMOROS, MEXICO

GARY PROVOST

POCKET BOOKS

New York   London   Toronto   Sydney   Tokyo

An *Original* Publication of POCKET BOOKS

POCKET BOOKS, a division of Simon & Schuster Inc.
1230 Avenue of the Americas, New York, NY 10020

ISBN: 0-671-69319-0

First Pocket Books printing September 1989

10 9 8 7 6 5 4 3 2 1

POCKET and colophon are trademarks of
Simon & Schuster Inc.

Printed in the U.S.A.

For all my
Writers Retreat Workshop students,
past and future.

Acknowledgments

I am grateful to many people whose cooperation and comfort helped make this book possible.

To my editor, Claire Zion, who would come last on the alphabetical list, I offer my first thanks. She sweated over every word with me, covered my ears when the clock was ticking too loudly, stayed up late, missed conferences, and moved with grace and diplomacy across that sometimes fragile line between a writer and his publisher.

I also want to thank: Israel Aldrete, Sara Aldrete, Juan Benitez, Jerry Brown, Steve Cascone, Ron Chepsiuk, Edith Eubanks, Robert Fiallo, Rita Foundray, Randy Freidus, Russ Galen, Patty Galvan, Isabel Hanson, Bill Huddleston, Gwen Huddleston, Trish Janeshutz, Robert Kahn, Lisa Kazmier, Arnold Levine, Margie Levine, Jack Loff, Rob MacGregor, Liz MacNamara, Hector Orozco, Teresita Pedraza, Federico Ponce-Rojas, Johanna Presto-Dominguez, Gail Provost, Dale Robertson, Peter Rubie, Mercedes Sandoval, Lynn Savino, Bea Scantlin, Leah Stewart, the Reverend Frank Strunk, Cherry Westcott, John Westcott, Judy Williams, Mark Williams, Keith Wilson, and Anthony Zavaleta.

A special thanks to Jim Budd of Mexico City, a real pro who came through when I needed him.

Contents

Foreword

It was a story that shocked the nation in April of 1989. Police had discovered the mutilated bodies of Texas college student Mark Kilroy and twelve others, along with evidence that the victims had been human sacrifices, ritualistically tortured and murdered. Four members of a satanic drug ring had been captured, but many more were at large. Among them were Adolfo Constanzo, a mysterious Cuban American from Miami who was said to be the gang's ringleader, and Sara Aldrete, a tall and attractive honor student at an American college who, it was said, lived a double life: friendly college girl by day, ritual killer by night. There was talk of Satanism, of cannibalism, of police payoffs, of more bodies buried in shallow graves. Much of this would turn out to be true.

Like most people, I was at once horrified and mesmerized by the news coverage of this story. There is something about the word "Satanism" and the idea of such rituals that make us all lean a little closer to our newspapers, and ask questions.

When I decided to write a book about the tragedy, I knew that I would have to write it fast. The terrible deaths in Matamoros were falling into the folklore of the Mexican countryside so rapidly that the facts had to be retrieved quickly, before they became indistinguishable from legend. I flew to Mexico and Texas. I visited the scenes and talked to the people. I wrung whatever information I could from whatever sources were available, and I ended up, as journalists inevitably do, with an intriguing, but imperfect, body of information. The answers to some of my questions had only been known by people who are now dead. The answers to others are in the minds of people who refused to talk to me. Memories were confused, temperaments were mercurial, and the bureaucracy was sometimes thick. Moreover, the murders had spawned rumors and had reinforced long-held superstitions.

Still, the answers to my questions came gradually forward and I have put them down here in a way that I hope unifies, enlarges, and finally, puts together in a clear and cohesive way all the scattered information that came our way in the press during April and May of 1989.

The legal machinery that will process this case will still be clanking along for months, even years, after this book is written. As I write, none of the suspects has been tried. Hence they are only suspects, and not convicted criminals. I in no way want to suggest that their guilt has been definitely established. Some of the suspects have confessed to crimes, but none of them have been tried in court and found guilty or not guilty. The crimes described in this book are alleged, and my description of them is based on reasonable conclusions derived from the facts I gathered from my own interviews, police reports, and media coverage. (The dialogue within scenes is based on the memories of interview subjects about what was said and who said it.)

Despite the difficulties in gathering and presenting the facts of this case, I believe it is important to do so. I am fascinated by the events in Matamoros and Mexico City. But beyond the details of the crime itself, I am fascinated by the impact that the story made on America's imagination. In April and May of 1989, everybody was talking about it. Americans seemed to have an urgent need to know more about it, and the question is, Why?

If you want to find out how important a story is to any group of newspaper readers, find the degree of identification, divide it by the distance from the reader, and multiply it by its relevance to the reader's life. That observation reflects the fact that the news is not just a blizzard of meaningless information. It is something powerful, something that is meaningful to us, moves us, touches our lives. We get personally involved with the stories we read and hear.

When I was researching this book and sifting through collected newspaper clippings about the massacre in what was being called "the killing fields" of Mexico, I kept this business of identification-distance-relevance in mind. I wondered why the story had been so big. I think that by examining that equation the answer can be found.

Identification? Well, there is Mark Kilroy, of course. American, white, someone's son. In virtually every story written during the first three days after the discovery, the disappearance of Mark Kilroy is rehashed. And of course, there is Sara Aldrete, who was at first reported to be an American citizen, and later a resident alien who attended school in America. Of course, Adolfo Constanzo was also an American citizen, just as much as Mark

Kilroy, but he is not someone most newspaper readers easily identified with. So there is an identification factor for Americans, but many of the people involved in the tragedy were Mexicans.

Distance? The events took place near the U.S. border, and it is certainly understandable that they got a lot of coverage in Texas. But why is the story so compelling in Alaska and New Jersey and Kansas? For most Americans it is a story that happened thousands of miles away.

So it seems to me that neither the identification factor nor the distance factor in this story is sufficient to explain the high degree of involvement Americans seem to have with it. It must be relevance. People must think this story has something to do with them.

Certainly drugs are relevant. There isn't a community in America that isn't agonizing over the drug problem. But still, drug stories are legion and you sure don't have to go to Mexico to find one. No, it isn't the drugs that Americans find so relevant. It is Satanism.

The events in Matamoros—real, proved, witnessed—gave a chilling answer to a question that had been haunting America for years. It is the question we ask when we see sensationalist movies, when we read bizarre newspaper articles, when we watch controversial television shows like Geraldo Rivera's special on Satanism. As the evidence crops up all around us, we can't help but wonder: Does this sort of thing really go on?

In Matamoros, an American nightmare came true.

Introduction

By Dr. Tony Zavaleta, Professor of Anthropology,
Southmost Texas College; City Commissioner,
Brownsville, Texas

Twenty years of experience as an anthropologist on the U.S.-Mexican border has taught me to expect the unusual, even the bizarre. But nothing could have prepared me for the grisly discovery, in April of 1989, that people were being ritually tortured and sacrificed in Matamoros, Mexico, just across the Rio Grande from Brownsville, Texas, where I live, teach, and serve as a city commissioner.

The tragedy that was uncovered by Mexican police touched the lives of many people in this area, in many ways. I found myself personally connected to the story in three ways: as a teacher, as a father, and as an expert on *curandismo,* the local border culture.

In my sociology class, where I lectured on social norms and deviancy, there had been one student, a rather nondescript young Mexican-American who had always seemed to struggle to pay attention. His name was Serafin Hernandez Garcia. He was a law enforcement major, and as the Matamoros story unfolded in the press, I learned that while this young man sat in my classroom, he was allegedly being groomed for initiation into a sinister cult that demanded blood sacrifices.

Another of my students was a young honor student named Sara Aldrete. Sara was the perfect student, intelligent, dedicated, interested. She was

15

an attractive and friendly young woman who greeted me with a smile every morning of the semester. Now on television and in the newspapers she was being called the "high priestess" of the cult, and police all over North and South America were hunting for her.

As a father, I felt the uneasiness that all parents felt when they heard about Mark Kilroy, the Texas college student who had been kidnapped, murdered, and mutilated by the cult. But perhaps I had a special level of identification. My son Tony was Mark's age. Like Mark, Tony was a student at the University of Texas. Like Mark, Tony was on spring break. Like Mark, Tony had spent much of his spring break in Matamoros. Furthermore, Tony had been in one of my anthropology classes with Sara Aldrete.

After the news of the terrible discovery broke, my son called me up.

"Dad," he said, "I just saw the news. Tell me this isn't happening. Tell me it's not true. Sara can't be involved in this thing. It can't be the same Sara. Is there some mistake?"

"There's no mistake," I told him.

"Dad," he said, "you know I was in Matamoros the night that Mark was kidnapped. I was near the place where they grabbed him. If Sara Aldrete had seen me that night and called me over or offered me a ride, I would have taken it."

My most public connection to the Matamoros cult killings story was in my role as anthropologist, specializing in the border culture. I have spent many years documenting that culture, and particularly the border folk medical and religious beliefs.

When the story broke, reporters, hungry for details about the culture that they thought had spawned these murders, called me.

Was it somehow related to any pre-Columbian tradition? they asked. Could it possibly be a revival of some ancient Aztec practice on the border?

The questions were disturbing. The intimation that these atrocities could be part of Mexican culture and in some way linked to Aztec practices was revolting to me.

"No," I told the first reporter who called, "I am absolutely certain that what we have here is not of Mexican origin. I seriously doubt that it could be in any way connected to Aztec traditions."

I would be repeating my answer for weeks on television and in newspaper interviews.

I told the reporters that the rites appeared to be some imported Afro-Caribbean tradition, something like Santeria, but not really Santeria, because that religion does not practice human sacrifice. More likely, what went on in secret over in Matamoros was part of Santeria's dark co-tradition of Palo Mayombe, and an aberrant form of it at that. Especially characteristic of Palo Mayombe was the evil cauldron, or nganga, that had been found. The nganga is the powerhouse of the mayombero, or Palo Mayombe priest.

Furthermore, I told them, this was consistent with some of my recent research. In the markets of Mexico City I had found considerable evidence of Caribbean witchcraft. In fact, in recent lectures at two Texas universities I had suggested to my audience that there was an encroachment of Afro-

Caribbean culture into northern Mexican witchcraft.

So what happened in Matamoros was not endemic to the culture of the area. Nonetheless, it was a shock to the culture. To the outsider, the distinctions are not so obvious, and the people of this area have been deeply wounded by the dreadful events.

But it is a wound that has already begun to heal.

Many people agree that if the cult had not decided to kill an American spring breaker, the cult would have rolled on, and would probably still be operating. They would have mounted a death toll rivaling the worst mass muderers. Many people that I have spoken to agree that Mark Kilroy's life was not wasted. They believe that by his death, others live.

Recently a *curandero,* a healer in the border culture, told me he was convinced that in life and death Mark Kilroy played a higher role. His death brought to an end, as the *curandero* put it, "the evil that has held our communities captive for the past several years."

I can't say for sure, and I don't claim to know about these things, but there are those who believe it to be so. Just as Adolfo Constanzo, the godfather of the cult, called upon the dark forces for his power, there are those in our community who invoke the power of good. Some people call them white witches, or *brujos blancos.* I've been talking to them a lot recently, and they say that things are better now. An evil has been removed from our border community. They say that things are going to get better.

A Note About Spanish Names

In Mexico, a person has a given name, followed by his father's surname, and then his mother's surname. Serafin Hernandez Garcia, for example, is the son of a man from the Hernandez family and a woman from the Garcia family. If you wanted to refer to Serafin by his last name, you would call him Hernandez or Hernandez Garcia, but never just Garcia, for that would imply that his father had disowned him or that his father was unknown.

"Criminals killed his body, but they were not able to kill his spirit. He is alive."

—Rev. Juan Nicolau, speaking at a memorial service for Mark Kilroy

"In their religion they believe in reincarnation. They believe their godfather will come back."

—A Mexican prosecutor

ONE

The Student

All Mark Kilroy wanted to do was have a good time on spring break.

It was March and he had labored through six difficult and dedicated months as a junior in the College of Natural Sciences at the University of Texas in Austin. He hadn't been a monk about it by any means. He had chased girls. He had cheered for the Longhorns. He had gotten seduced into games of three-on-three basketball when he could have been studying. And occasionally he had put his books aside and fled to the freedom of Sixth Street, a honky-tonk area of downtown Austin, where he sometimes got drunk on beer.

But on the whole Mark hadn't done much partying, certainly not a lot for a tall, good-looking, fun-loving twenty-one-year-old. By far the thing in his life he gave most attention to during the spring of 1989 was his studies. From September to March, Mark plowed through the sometimes ponderous books with the determination of a donkey. He was carrying eighteen credits and had already gained a reputation as a serious student who usually put schoolwork ahead of his social life. It was important to Mark that he do well. Maturity was gaining on him rapidly. A year earlier he had finally decided what he wanted to do with his life. He wanted to go to medical school. He wanted to be a doctor.

On Friday, March 10, as he stood in his small apartment near the downtown campus, stuffing T-shirts and shorts and sneakers into a garment bag, perhaps he thought: I deserve this. I've studied like a maniac, I deserve a good time.

The good time that Mark had in mind was something he had talked about constantly for weeks. Mark had carried on about spring break like a five-year-old trying to rush Christmas morning. He had squirreled away spending money from his food allowance. A couple of times a week he had discussed spring break on the phone with his high school friend Bradley Moore, a junior at Texas A&M University in College Station, Texas, who was majoring in electrical engineering. And to anyone who would listen, Mark had outlined his plans with such enthusiasm that it seemed that Mark, himself, was hearing it for the first time.

"Here's the plan," he told them.

Mark, Bradley Moore, Bill Huddleston, and Brent Martin would drive down the Texas Gulf Coast to South Padre Island, near Brownsville. None of the other guys were UT students. Brent Martin, twenty, was a sophomore at Alvin Community College in Alvin, Texas. (Alvin, next to Santa Fe, Texas, which is the boys' hometown, is best known as the home of baseball star Nolan Ryan.) Bill Huddleston, twenty-one, was a junior at Texas A&M in Galveston, majoring in engineering and business management. So it would be a kind of a reunion. It would be the way it was back in '85 and '86 when the four of them were high school pals in Santa Fe, Texas. Mark had played on the baseball team with Bill Huddleston. He had been on the basketball team with Moore and Martin. This was going to be great. They would drink beer. Soak up rays. Talk sports. Meet girls.

South Padre, famous for its surfing, its fishing, and its warm and sunny winters, is a natural magnet for Texas college students. "Texas Week" in March, when 300,000 young men and women inject about ten million dollars into the local economy, is the biggest week of the year for the restaurants and hotels in the area. Besides its beaches and the presence of the opposite sex in great bathing-suited numbers, South Padre Island is attractive to students because of its nearness to Mexico, where beer is plentiful and nobody asks for an ID.

Though this was to be the first trip to South Padre Island for Martin, Moore, and Huddleston, Mark had been there before. He had gone twice with other friends. But this trip was special. Mark knew that this summer after his junior year would probably be the last one that he and his pals would spend together in Santa Fe. In a way it was their last chance to be kids. After senior year, who knew what would happen? The winds of life would scatter them in all directions. Graduate schools, careers, marriages, and children would all pry loose the bonds of friendship that had been made strong by the less complex issues of adolescence. Certainly they would all see each other again. But Mark was mature enough to know that time had a way of shifting priorities, and if he didn't know it, he perhaps sensed that this spring break with the guys, drenched in that certain exuberance, that mood and texture that is peculiar to young, single males on the loose, would be the last of its kind. So this spring break was special for that. And it was also special, he must have thought as he finished packing, because they were finally going to Mexico. On his other trips to South Padre he had never crossed the border into Mexico. He had always wanted to go, and this time for sure the guys were determined to drive down to Brownsville and cross the bridge into Matamoros.

At two o'clock on Friday afternoon, Bradley Moore showed up. Mark was already packed.

Moore has been badly shaken by Mark's death and except for a few general comments, has chosen not to talk to the press publicly. However, we can easily imagine the exuberance of the moment when he picked up Mark for their trip.

"Let's get you packed and move south," Moore might have said.

Mark would smile. "I'm all packed, turkey."

"You need some help with your things?"

"Hey, get serious." Mark was a strong, athletic young man, and in the brazen way of college kids he probably hoisted the bag with one hand and carried it out.

Mark tossed his bag into Bradley Moore's car and the two young men began the 150-mile drive from Austin to Santa Fe, where they would visit their families and then pick up the other two members of their spring-break squad, who would already be home, visiting families.

It would be the last time Mark's UT friends would see him. One of them, senior Frank Padula, spoke later about Mark to Siva Vaidhyanathan of the *Dallas Morning News*.

Vaidhyanathan writes:

"Mr. Padula said he saw Mr. Kilroy the day he left on his trip. 'He said to me, "We've got to get together soon, man, we've got to have a good time."'

"Mr. Padula said he told Mr. Kilroy that he had been having trouble with math and had not been very active socially.

"'The last thing he said to me was, "When I get back, I'm going to help you with that math course and you're going to pass it,"' Mr. Padula said. 'I said, "I'd do anything for you, I'll even pay you."'

"'Mr. Kilroy responded, "No, just buy me a six-pack,"' Mr. Padula said. 'He had a heart; this guy had a heart.'"

Along the way to Sante Fe with Moore, Mark talked mostly about school. He told Moore how much he was enjoying life at UT and Austin. Mark, who had turned twenty-one on March 1, was in particularly high spirits because he would not have to spend his vacation counting pennies after all. His parents had called and told him they would pay for the trip, as a birthday present.

By eleven that night Mark and Bradley reached Santa Fe. At one A.M. Mark hugged his parents and his nineteen-year-old brother, Keith, good-bye for the last time and the fellows piled into Brent Martin's car. They drove south through the flat plains of East Texas. It was landscape they knew well, one where farms and ranches big enough to contain entire cities stretched to every horizon during the day. But the field of vision on this night was decidedly un-Texan. The darkness closed around them like a glove, and the beams of Martin's headlights were tossed back at them by walls of fog. The world had been reduced to four guys in a car.

While Brent drove, the boys probably talked about the things young men talk about: school, sports, girls. No doubt they traded war stories from the battle of the sexes, and they laughed.

At ten A.M. on Saturday, March 11, weary from the long drive, the four young men arrived at the Sheraton Hotel on South Padre Island.

In the hotel there were other students, mostly from the Southwest, and as Mark walked across the lobby with his friends, perhaps he could sense that he was part of a growing wave of college kids filling the town. Spring break in South Padre was a happening and he was part of it. He might have stretched his long arms and legs to get out the kinks from the long drive.

Too excited to sleep, the boys went out to eat, then they spent much of the morning by the water. "We walked on the beach," Bill Huddleston recalls. And as they walked, perhaps Mark could feel the tension from all those months of studying flow from his body. To Mark, it probably seemed that school was sometimes a pressure cooker, but that someday it would all be worth it.

Despite their lack of sleep the boys were determined to have a big night out. In the afternoon, after checking out the Miss Tanline contest behind the hotel, they tried to nap in their rooms.

"For the next two days it was the same procedure," Huddleston says. "We went to the beach, walked around, saw the Tanline contest, and towards the latter part of the afternoon when the sun was coming down, we'd go back to the room, clean up, hang around, go get something to eat. We'd try to take a nap, but it never worked. We'd be just sort of calm and relaxed, just trying to settle down, fixing to get ready to go out at night."

Spring break was in full swing by this time on South Padre, and the common denominator, it seemed, was beer. In front of the Sailorman's Pub someone stole a van carrying fifteen kegs of Budweiser. (The van and two of the kegs of beer were later recovered.) In another incident, three young men were fined for trying to steal three cases of Miller Lite twelve-ounce cans from the back of a beer truck. A Houston man was injured when he fell two stories from his condominium while trying to steal a keg of beer from an adjoining balcony. And the owners of the Palmetto Inn reported the theft of three kegs of Michelob Light, and four cases of Löwenbräu from a walk-in cooler. So there was, as there always is when kids gather for spring break, a sense of mischief in the air. But if Mark and his friends thought about it at all, they must have thought there was nothing the least bit dangerous about partying on spring break.

On Sunday night, after two full days in South Padre, the boys went to Matamoros for the first time with four girls from the University of Kansas, whom they had met at a drive-in hamburger joint in Port Isabel. Port Isabel, on the way to Brownsville, is south of South Padre Island, just across the Laguna Madre. It was a great night of drinking and carousing, and they went back to the hotel vowing to return to Matamoros the next night.

On Monday night, March 13, the boys went again to Mexico. They parked Martin's car in Brownsville and walked to the International Gateway Bridge, which leads to Mexico.

Brownsville, just across the causeway from Port Isabel, and 135 miles south of Corpus Christi, is the southernmost city in the continental United States. It sits on the Rio Grande in the heart of the area of southern Texas known as the Rio Grande Valley, and it is the county seat of Cameron County. With a population of 115,000, 80 percent of them of Spanish descent, it is the largest city on the southern border. Brownsville, which survives on oil, natural gas, farming, tourism, and shrimping, prides itself on being Texas's "second most historic city," right behind San Antonio. Being a border town, Brownsville is heavily populated with Mexicans and Mexican-Americans. The downtown storefronts are painted a variety of bright colors, more typical of Spanish-speaking cultures than

American, and most of the signs on downtown stores are in Spanish.

At the American customs gate leading into Mexico, one of the guards asked Mark two questions. They were the same two questions they ask everybody.

"What country is your citizenship?"

"U.S.A.," Mark answered.

"What is your business in Mexico?"

"Fun," he probably said.

The guard waved him on.

The sidewalks of the International Gateway Bridge were jammed with people. Still, Mark and his friends moved at a faster clip than the cars, which were practically at a standstill. The bridge, which is three blocks long, is the easiest link between the U.S. and Mexico for thousands of people who work in one country and live in the other. With the additional tourists, traffic would be heavy on the bridge all through spring break. When Mark looked over the bridge railing, he was staring at the Rio Grande (or the Rio Bravo, which is what the Mexicans call it), which at that point at that time of year was hardly more than a puddle between the two countries.

They walked into Mexico, four boys full of themselves, looking for girls and beer.

As you come off the International Bridge into Matamoros, you enter a wide, circular plaza. There is a rotary of traffic going from, and coming to, the bridge. The perimeter of the rotary is a sidewalk for the thousands of people who move between

Brownsville and Matamoros by foot. And in the middle of the rotary is a small park where tour guides hawk their services and Mexican vendors sell food and Cokes from wagons.

On the other side of the plaza is the Avenido Obregon, with its strip of bars that offer hot Mexican food and cold Mexican beer.

Matamoros, which is described in the popular guidebook *Texas* (APA Productions, 1986) as "one of the cleanest and most appealing cities on the border," is a hotbed of farmworker activism and political turmoil. The city had recently gone through a period of reform. The red light district has been put out of business. The new police commander, Juan Benitez, was developing a reputation for toughness and honesty. And the authorities were cracking down on immigrant smugglers and dope smugglers. Beyond the tourist district are hundreds of tight, heavily populated blocks of small houses, and beyond the city itself is a checkerboard of farms and ranches along the Rio Bravo.

The boys crossed the wide plaza at the foot of the bridge. Mexican cabdrivers called in English to tourists, urging them to visit the shopping district. Pushcart vendors sold barbecued chicken from smoky grills. Shop owners offered great deals on souvenirs, "For your mama."

Mark must have liked Matamoros. It wasn't like other Mexican border towns where blanket peddlers dog your every step and American franchises call themselves El this and El that. This wasn't like some Mexican pavilion at a World's Fair in Nebraska. This was the real thing.

Still, as he and the others pushed their way through the crowds along the main street, the Avenido Obregon, it would be easy for Mark to feel as if he were still in the U.S.A. Most of the faces around him were American. They were college kids, thousands of young men and women packed, in Bill Huddleston's words, "belly to belly." Like Mark, they were looking for a good time and maybe hoping to meet someone special.

Along the avenue Mexican vendors had erected sandwich signs promising the best possible price on margaritas and beer. Several of the bars had been renamed to appeal to the kids. There was the Hard Rock Cafe, Sergeant Pepper's, even one called Cheers.

They worked their way through the crowd to a bar called Los Sombreros. From there they went to the Hard Rock Cafe, which had been The London Pub until the American kids arrived.

Once inside, Mark could hardly hear himself think. It was a boisterous place, dramatically over-crowded. The music blared. Kids howled and hooted. Mark and the others huddled at the bar, thinking they'd like to meet girls but not sure they could even strike up a conversation in such a madhouse.

It was Mark who got lucky. He fell into a conversation with a group of girls, eventually working it down to one, a young lady named Stephanie, whom he had seen earlier at the Miss Tanline contest, where she had finished third. Stephanie and Mark wedged their way out of the bar and into the street where they could talk better. The frat-party atmosphere extended out onto the sidewalks, where students were drinking beer from cans and wine from plastic glasses, and some kids were openly smoking joints. But at least Mark and Stephanie had gotten away from the music and they could talk.

Mark told Stephanie, perhaps, about Austin and the grueling semester he had just endured. They must have agreed that college was great, but it could damn near kill you.

By two o'clock in the morning everybody was running out of steam. Mark took Stephanie's hand and led her through the thinning crowd back to her friends. He and his pals, all slightly soused, began the four-block walk back to the bridge.

"We crossed over from the club we were in," Huddleston remembers, "and as we were walking back, I was more or less in back and Bradley and Brent were in the middle and Mark was in front. We weren't side by side, but we were still in a kind of group more or less within ten yards of each other. Then Mark came back to me and asked me what was wrong, because I wasn't really in a party mood that night. Mark was like that, he would ask you what was wrong. He was the kind of guy that always put other people before himself. He wanted to know how come I wasn't acting like the other guys. I wanted to, but we had partied and partied and I just was worn out. Physically, I wasn't in a party mood. I told Mark everything was just fine, I was just kind of mellow. So we just started walking back again in our group, and then I had to use the rest room, so I had made up my mind I was going to go behind a tree up ahead near Garcia's. I started walking faster, so I could get ahead of them, and made like a beeline so I could go behind the tree and hopefully meet up with them just past Garcia's, which is exactly what happened. I thought Mark was with Bradley and Brent all this time, but he wasn't. They were walking along, checking out the sights, looking at girls, you know, and so Mark was behind everybody at the time, and I guess around Garcia's was where he met the guy in the truck."

Garcia's is a popular Matamoros restaurant and souvenir store, just across the plaza from the International Gateway Bridge. Next to Garcia's there is a small and narrow parking lot where earlier in the night Mexican vendors had loitered, hoping to wring a few final dollars out of American tourists before they crossed the bridge. It seems that what happened to Mark Kilroy in front of Garcia's is that he heard someone calling to him. We can imagine what happened afterward, based on the statements of Serafin Hernandez Garcia and other suspects.

Mark turned to see who it was. Across the parking lot there was a young Hispanic man leaning against a pickup truck. (This was Hernandez Garcia.) Not wanting to be unfriendly, Mark walked closer.

"What's that?" he asked.

"I said would you like to go for a ride?" the man said.

"Where to?" Mark asked.

"Come here," the man said. "I'll tell you."

Mark, his senses probably dulled by alcohol, walked closer.

When Mark got close, the young man, who had been speaking only English, shouted something in Spanish. Suddenly there were two of them, strong young Mexican men who jumped out of the truck. They grabbed Mark, pinned his arms behind him. They dragged him toward the truck.

"Hey, what the hell are you doing?" Mark shouted.

He kicked at them. He tried to butt them with his head. But they were too strong.

"What do you want? Who do you think I am? You've got the wrong guy."

He tried, perhaps, to fight them off with some of the moves he had learned in karate class at UT, but the alcohol in him and their combined strength would have been just too much. They pushed him into the truck and held him there while one of the men got behind the wheel and sped out of the parking lot.

What the hell was going on? Mark must have thought. Why would somebody kidnap him? His parents didn't have money. These people didn't even know who he was. This was crazy.

"It's okay, don't worry," one of the Hispanic men said.

Was this some sort of prank? Where were Bill and Brent and Bradley?

"What's going on?" he cried. "Just tell me that, what are you going to do with me?"

"Just shut up," he was told.

The truck went a few blocks and then stopped.

The driver got out. As near as Mark could probably tell, the driver had just stopped to take a piss. Mark leaned back, as if to accept his capture, then he lunged for the door, pushed it open, and threw himself out. He heard the men behind him shouting in Spanish. He stood up and started running. He was an athlete, he could run. *I can outrun them,* he must have thought. *I can outrun them.* He ran hard, his feet pounding on the pavement, his heart racing. He ran as fast as he could. But in a moment he must have realized it was not just the young men chasing him. There was a car. *God,* he must have thought, *there are more of them.* The car swerved in front of him. Two more young Mexican men got out. They ran at him. They banged into him, knocking his breath away. They held him down and pinned his arms behind his back, then dragged him to the car. His skin must have tingled with fear. He must have wanted to cry, feeling so helpless. The men pushed him into the backseat of the car. One of them tied Mark's hands behind his back.

This is more or less what police believe happened that night, and as the car pulled away, Mark must have screamed at them to tell him what was going on, but they ignored him. The car drove through the dark back streets of Matamoros. Gradually the houses and shops disappeared and were replaced by fields. They were outside the city, driving through farmland. It was bizarre, he must have thought. These Mexicans were young guys, just like his pals. But they were crazy or something. What the hell were they going to do with him?

After a half hour or so the car pulled off the

highway and onto a long dirt road. Mark must have peered out at the darkness and seen that they were on a farm. The car pulled to a stop near an old equipment barn. He was taken into the barn, with his arms tied behind his back. His legs were tied and he was gagged. Then the men left him. There was silence. He was trapped in the barn. In the dark. In a foreign country. Probably, he cried.

All night long Mark stayed in the barn. He must have worn his wrists raw struggling to escape. He must have played over and over in his mind all of the possible scenarios that could explain his desperate situation. He must have glanced around, hoping to see reflections from the lights of a police car. He must have listened for the sounds of friends who had found him. There must have been times of deep, sickening panic when he was sure that these strange foreign men were going to kill him. There must have been times when the terror was so great that he told himself no, they just want ransom money for me, or they just want to scare me, or they want me to help them get into America. Something. Anything. He must have felt terror. He must have prayed.

In the morning another man, much older and gentler than the youths who had abducted Mark, came and gave him food. Mark must have considered it a hopeful sign. He tried to make the man help him, but without success. By two o'clock in the afternoon Mark had been moved to an old swinging hammock on the farm, where he lay, still gagged and with his hands and legs still tied behind him. About that time one of the young men and another man, someone Mark had not seen before, came for him.

"Are you going to hurt me?" he asked.

"No," he was told.

Thick, heavy tape was placed over his eyes and his mouth. With his hands still cuffed behind his back, he was led along. The earth beneath his feet was soft. Soon the light just beyond the tape was lost and he knew he'd been taken inside, a barn or a shed or something. The place smelled something awful, as if it were filled with rotting hay and animal carcasses. He was pushed down until his body was flat, his face in the dirt. Endless seconds passed. He heard the new man speaking in Spanish. In a moment he felt a sudden and excruciating burning pain come into his head.

Hopefully, he never quite realized until that moment that he was going to die.

TWO

The Search

Bill Huddleston, like the others, was tall, good-looking, and a good student. And like Kilroy, Martin, and Moore, he had been an athlete in a town that places a high value on high school athletics. Huddleston and the others were in many ways perfect reflections of the town of Santa Fe, Texas. Just a few thousand souls on Texas Highway 6 between Houston and Galveston, Santa Fe is friendly, wholesome, middle class, a town with one main street, one high school. It is a town that is firmly welded to basic American values.

Huddleston was also Mark Kilroy's closest friend.

Today, Bill Huddleston is as deeply scarred by the events in Matamoros as his buddies Martin and Moore. The tragedy has pushed him into adulthood, forced him to scrutinize more closely the meaning of his life.

"I'll be trying a little harder to succeed, to be a good person," says Huddleston, who still has a close friendship with Mark's younger brother, Keith. "I feel I owe it to Mark. Mark had a great impact on me. He gave me a lot of advice. We were real close. Everything I do, I'll be thinking of Mark in some way."

While Brent Martin and Bradley Moore have chosen not to speak about the tragedy, Huddleston and his family believe, says his mother, Gwen, "that Bill needs to talk about it."

He remembers that first night well.

"That night after we saw Mark was gone, I walked back a few blocks to see if he was there," he says. "Then Brent and Bradley headed across the border to see if Mark went back to the car. After I didn't find Mark, I met them at the car and we drove around just asking people, 'Hey, did you see our friend?' And there was this guy who had gone to Texas A&M, and he had grown up in Brownsville and he offered to take me back over to Matamoros in his truck and look around.

"So we drove over. Brent and Bradley stayed on the Texas side in case Mark showed up. We went over and the vendors were all leaving, everybody had pretty much cleared out and it was dead. The guy spoke Spanish real well and we went upstairs in this one club that was the only one still open. We checked it out and Mark wasn't there. Then we saw a Mexican policeman and this guy went over, speaking Spanish to him, and asking him to call in on the radio to see if maybe Mark had gotten picked up and was in one of the cells.

"Nothing turned up, so we left. It was around four-thirty, hours after everybody had left. So I went back and met Bradley and Brent and we talked it over and we thought, well, maybe Mark went home with the girl or her friends or something, and we went back to the hotel.

"The next morning when we woke up, I guess it was early afternoon, and we hadn't had a phone call or anything from Mark, that's when we knew that something was really wrong. So we went over to Matamoros to the American consulate and we talked to this guy, Michael O'Keefe. He contacted the hospitals, the jails, all the places Mark could possibly be, but everybody said, no, Mark wasn't there. So Mr. O'Keefe gave us his number, so we could keep in touch, and he said he'd call us if they heard anything.

"We went back to South Padre Island, still discussing what possibly could have happened. We went to the police there on South Padre, and they were the ones that suggested we call the Kilroys that night. See, we didn't want to get Mark's parents all stirred up in case it turned out to be no big deal. But the police thought it was a good idea to call them. So we talked it over, who was going to be the one to call them, so I decided I'd do it. I talked to his mom, his dad was out of town."

This was Tuesday, March 14.

Though the Kilroys spoke to the press dozens of times during the crisis, afterward they refused to make public statements. As a result, while much of what they did during those troubling days after Mark disappeared is well documented, most of what they felt is not.

Certainly they must have gone through the inevitable litany of possibilities. Mark had been kidnapped, Mark was lost, Mark had fallen down and was hurt, Mark had amnesia. And there must have been moments when they simply stared into each other's eyes and gave no words to the most troubling possibility of all. The Kilroys are a devout Roman Catholic family, so certainly they prayed.

They decided that Helen would stay in Santa Fe, at least for the time being, and Jim Kilroy would go to Brownsville.

By the time Mark's father got to Brownsville, the investigation had come into the hands of Oran Neck, special agent in charge of the U.S. Customs Service investigations office. Neck, forty-five, is an affable, no-nonsense Texas lawman. Stocky, balding, and bespectacled, he looks like a younger version of the Quaker Oats spokesman, Wilford Brimley.

"Jim Kilroy contacted his brother Ken," Neck says, "and Ken called me. It happened that I know Ken Kilroy, he's a customs agent in Los Angeles. We decided that one thing we should do is contact George Gavito." Big, dark-skinned, and quick with a quip, Gavito is the deputy sheriff for Cameron County.

Neck has fifty agents under him, but their cases rarely involve missing people. "Most of what we do involves contraband, illegal drugs, that sort of thing," he says. So Gavito was a logical person to turn to.

"Gavito had already gotten a report on the disappearance from the South Padre police," Neck says. "George and I decided to do a joint investigation. It's kind of hard to explain, but when a kid is missing in Mexico the U.S. police agencies don't really have any jurisdiction, so we took it on as a personal involvement."

This "personal involvement" would turn out to be the most publicized case of Neck's career. For the next month he would be eating, sleeping, and breathing the Mark Kilroy investigation, and even after Mark was found it would be Neck more than anybody else whom reporters would turn to for information.

Neck had decided right from the beginning that if he was going to find Mark Kilroy, he would need the press.

"We wanted to get this investigation to the highest levels of public attention," he says. "Sometimes there is a tendency for these things to be kind of swept under the table. We didn't want that to happen."

On Wednesday, March 15, the day after he found out about the disappearance, Neck took *Brownsville Herald* reporter Lisa Baker and photographer Brad Doherty over to Matamoros, along with Martin, Moore, and Huddleston, and the group traced Mark Kilroy's last known steps. The next day the *Herald* ran a front-page story with photos about the missing college student.

"We knew that these spring breakers who had been in town when Mark disappeared would only be around for a week or so, so we wanted to get the word out fast, in case anybody had seen anything," Neck says. "After the *Herald* ran the story, the radio and television stations picked it up. After that we tried to talk to the press every day, keep the story in the public eye, and the press bent over backwards to help us."

The story was important to the local press because tourism is a big part of the economy for both the Brownsville area and Matamoros. Kids had been reported missing on spring break before, dozens of them every year, but in the past they had always staggered home with a hangover, or been bailed out of a Mexican jail after getting arrested for some drunken escapade. The longer Mark was missing, the more damage it would do to the local tourist trade.

Also, Mark's disappearance came at a particularly tender moment in Mexican-American relations. Mexico's $100 billion foreign debt, illegal Mexican immigration, drugs and corruption, and the slowness of democratic reforms were all issues that ignited sparks between the two countries. The press was anxious to see if the two neighbors could cooperate long enough to find the missing college student.

In the days that followed, Oran Neck would also meet with Juan Benitez Ayala, commandant of the Mexican Federal Judicial Police in Matamoros. Benitez, thirty-five, was a nine-year veteran of the force but had only been at the Matamoros job for a couple of months. He was, says Neck, "the new kid on the block."

These three, Neck, Gavito, and Benitez, would head up the search for Mark Kilroy. While Benitez handled things on the Mexican side of the Rio Grande, Neck and Gavito worked side by side, sometimes literally.

"I just moved into Gavito's office," Neck says. "We made that headquarters for the search."

On Wednesday, the fifteenth, Bill Huddleston and the American lawmen gathered in George Gavito's office with a professional hypnotist who had helped the sheriff's office on other cases. Neck and the others were hoping that Huddleston was carrying around in his subconscious some detail that could aid the investigation.

Under hypnosis, Huddleston remembered that before he had gone ahead of his friends to take a leak behind the tree, Kilroy had stopped to talk to a young Mexican man.

"Hey, don't I know you from somewhere?" the young man had said.

The young Mexican man, as Huddleston remembered, was thin, about five feet eight, and wore a blue plaid shirt and light-colored pants. He also had a circular wound on his face. The wound had not healed. It was fresh.

That was all Huddleston could remember.

Though this mysterious man with the wound on his face would occupy the minds of the investigators, it seems now that he was an irrelevancy, just some guy who happened to be there at a significant moment. There is no evidence that this man has a connection to Mark's kidnapping.

The police also pressed Bradley Moore for his memories of the girl Mark had been talking to, but Moore knew little except that her name was Stephanie and that she had been a contestant in the Miss Tanline contest on South Padre. Besides, Moore said, it didn't matter. He was convinced that his buddy would not have gone off with a girl that night, no matter how enticing the invitation might have been.

"There's no way he left with somebody else," Moore told them. "Something has happened. I've known the guy ever since kindergarten. He wouldn't go off and just not call. We had come out of [the bar] and walked away, and when we turned around to say 'Where's Mark?' he was gone, and that's the last we've seen of him. He was drunk, we were drunk, and we lost him.'"

"We had agents scour each one of the tanline contests," Neck says. "There were fifteen or twenty of them at the different hotels and we found the girl.'"

Stephanie, however, had nothing to add to what the police already knew.

Within a few days of the disappearance, police in Brownsville and Matamoros had been given pictures of Mark Kilroy, and it became a matter of policy that with each arrest, suspects were asked, "Have you seen this boy?"

On Thursday, March 16, Jim Kilroy arrived in Brownsville, offering a $5,000 reward for information leading to his son's whereabouts.

Kilroy passed out posters with Mark's picture on them. Sometimes with one of Neck's agents, other times on his own or with the boys, he walked the streets of Matamoros. For days he retraced Mark's footsteps over and over, perhaps thinking that somehow if he just did it right or often enough he could figure out what had happened to his son. He must have walked endlessly in the circle of the main plaza with its cabdrivers, tour guides, and pushcart vendors. He showed Mark's picture to everyone.

"Have you seen this boy?"

"No," he was told.

He walked along the Avenido Obregon, weaving his way through the tourists. He went to the Hard Rock Cafe, to Sergeant Pepper's, to Garcia's. He walked down the side streets of Matamoros, into the tight, crowded, noisy neighborhoods.

On Saturday, March 18, Lieutenant Gavito enlisted the help of U.S. Border Patrol agents to search the Rio Grande area in helicopters and four-wheel-drive vehicles. Jim Kilroy and two of Mark's friends spent the day posting flyers with Mark's picture throughout Matamoros and Brownsville, and they handed them to tourists at the bridge.

On Sunday, March 19, Palm Sunday, Jim Kilroy met with Bishop John Joseph Fitzpatrick of the Brownsville diocese. Through Bishop Fitzpatrick, Kilroy asked priests in Matamoros to spread the word about Mark's disappearance in their church services.

Mark had grown up in a religous Roman Catholic household, and perhaps his father thought that if his son were in trouble and saw a church, he might go to it. No doubt a good many memories of moments with Mark came back to Mr. Kilroy, and one that he shared with the press concerned Mark's

Bible reading at times when he was supposed to be doing his high school studies.

"But what are you going to do," Jim said to reporters, "bawl a kid out for reading the Bible?"

At the churches, the answer was the same as it was at the hospitals and the jails. No one had seen Jim Kilroy's son.

He must have read the newspapers, thinking there would be a clue. He must have hoped for something. Anything.

Certainly during this time there were provocative stories that could have made his blood run faster, made him sit up and pull the newspaper page close to his face.

There was, for example, a story in the *Brownsville Herald* about a Matamoros "coyote." That's what they call a man who smuggles immigrants. The coyote, according to the story, paid police officers to apprehend Central Americans who were planning to sneak into the United States. The immigrants, allegedly, were sold to the coyote as hostages for $50 each. The coyote would then ask the hostage for $350. If the hostage could have the money sent from family back home, the coyote would take him to the river and tell him how to get safely across. If the hostage could not come up with the money, he was put to work for fifteen days carrying sand and making tile and concrete for the magnificent house that the coyote was building in an exclusive section of Matamoros, one mile from the bridge.

The story might have shown Kilroy how easily a person could disappear in Matamoros. The story also reflected the widely held belief that Mexican police, like some of the handmade goods along the Avenido Obregon, could be bought at bargain prices.

Jim Kilroy traveled back and forth between Santa Fe and Brownsville all through March and the beginning of April.

"Jim Kilroy was with us all the time," Neck says. "After my initial meeting with Gavito we set up our little thing over in the sheriff's office, and on the days when Kilroy was in Brownsville, he must have spent eighteen or twenty hours a day there. He worked with us, he ate with us, he'd go out and hang up posters and come back. He was part of the investigating team."

Because of Oran Neck's efforts at keeping the Kilroy story in the press, and because of the general feeling that the disappearance of an American student in Mexico was one more thorn in the side of already troubled Mexican-American relations, everybody wanted the case cleared up quickly. So it got a lot of attention.

In Mexico the Federal Judicial Police and the State Judicial Police assigned ten full-time investigators to the case. In Texas, Gavito asked the attorney general for more state troopers and he got them.

The Texas police rousted Brownsville criminals and other lowlifes. "We had a new lead every day," Neck says.

The Mexican police swept through Matamoros's shantytowns for clues to the disappearance. The poverty-stricken areas along the river were known to be high-crime areas, and some of the people who lived in the barrios frequented the Avenido Obregon, where, it was said, they preyed on American tourists. Hundreds of criminals were picked up and questioned. Helicopters swooped over the banks of the Rio Grande. Leads were followed. Rumors investigated. Nothing.

Though Jim Kilroy must have wanted every resource, every man-hour, dedicated to the search for Mark, a reading of the daily paper would have shown him that the police on both sides of the border had their normal ration of crime to deal with, and the Gateway Bridge seemed to be near a lot of it. During the two weeks following Mr. Kilroy's arrival in Brownsville, an eighteen-year-old UT student on her way from a nightclub back to the international bridge was gang-raped by four men. A Mexican truck driver was robbed and stabbed to death while waiting to pass through Mexican customs on the bridge. Dean Scott, another UT student, was beaten and robbed near the bridge by a Texas boy and a Mexican. And a night watchman at a Matamoros car wash died in a shootout with assailants ten blocks east of the bridge.

Not surprisingly, tourism was down in Matamoros, and many of those tourists who did go into the city were extra cautious. Some women removed jewelry before entering Matamoros. Others left their pocketbooks behind in Brownsville. Merchants in Matamoros were distressed, and they were as anxious as everybody else to have the American found. Kilroy's disappearance was bad for business.

For Jim Kilroy, the most difficult moments of each day must have been when he called home to tell Helen there was no news. Helen was by the phone constantly, and whenever it rang, she must have felt a surge of hope that Mark had been found.

"I have not left the phone since the day the boys called me to let me know about Mark," Helen, a volunteer paramedic with the Santa Fe Emergency Medical Service, told the press. "I have been praying and praying for his return," she said.

In fact, there did come a night, about a week after Mark disappeared, when the phone rang and it did bring a moment's hope.

The conversation went something like this:

"Hello."

"Mrs. Kilroy?" a man said.

"Yes."

"We have your son, Mrs. Kilroy."

"What? Who is this? You have Mark, is he okay?"

"He's fine. You can have him back, but it will cost you."

Even then Helen must have known that something was wrong, kidnappers calling after all this time. The disappearance had been widely covered in the press. Anybody could call and say they had Mark. But still . . .

The man demanded $10,000. He told Mrs. Kilroy where to deliver the money, and he told her that if she let the police in on it, he would cut off Mark's fingers and mail them to her. There were other calls, some from a different man. According to the Associated Press, Mrs. Kilroy tried to pay the initial $2,000, but the pickup was never made. Eventually police arrested Robert George Miller and Wilton Joseph Smith, along with Elmer Ranferi Corado, Becky Rita Smith, and Mardoquoro Zamora Gonzalez, all allegedly accomplices.

Miller and Smith were in the Galveston County jail when they allegedly made the phone calls to Mrs. Kilroy. They had telephones in their cells. A Galveston deputy later explained to the press that inmates had telephones in their cells to be used to contact family members or their attorneys. They could make collect calls only. The deputy added, somewhat cryptically, that putting telephones in cells was "the most practical system in a jail built to hold three hundred inmates."

If there were a few people trying to cash in on the Kilroys' tragedy, there were many more who were there to help. The Kilroys had put up $5,000 as reward money for the safe return of Mark, but the reward was increased to $15,000 when a combine of fifteen to twenty Brownsville businesspeople offered to put up $10,000 more to help solve the case.

The money that the Kilroys had raised for a reward was eventually donated to indigent people in Matamoros.

In Santa Fe, where neighbors of the Kilroys planned fund-raisers to help finance the search, the person most devoted to helping find Mark, outside of the Kilroy family, was Gwen Huddleston, Bill's mother. Mrs. Huddleston, who teaches music and theater arts at her Santa Fe studio, had known Helen Kilroy mainly as "Bill's friend's mother," but the crisis brought the women closer together.

"As soon as I found out what was going on, I was willing to go right down there," she says. "But Billy said, 'No, Mom, we're handling it all right, no need to come down.' All the boys insisted on staying down there for a while, even though the other parents wanted them to come back. When Helen's choice was not to go down, we started a campaign right here, organizing flyers, and so forth. I knew it had to get out on the media. If you didn't have the news, you weren't going to find him; Mark was going to be just another missing person.

"I worked just about around the clock, doing phone calls, I worked with 'America's Most Wanted,' I sent flyers down to Brownsville for them to pass out.

"I don't think there was ever a moment during that whole time when I felt that we weren't going to find him. I personally felt that he was over in Mexico and that he was probably in a prison over there, taken hostage or something by one of their police officials. Even as time went on I still felt that we were going to find him."

By the time Mark had been missing for a week, thousands of flyers had been sent down and spread around the Rio Grande Valley. Still no word on Mark, and it was far too late for Mrs. Kilroy to believe that Mark was simply lost. In her private thoughts and in the statements she made to reporters, it seems, she was moving inexorably toward the conclusion that a tragedy of monstrous proportions had struck her family.

On March 20 she told a reporter, "I've really felt strongly that somehow he's being hurt right now."

She said that she firmly believed that someone was holding her son against his will.

"It doesn't matter now what has happened to him," she said. "We just want him back. I don't hold any anger against anybody."

In her daily Bible reading and her praying Helen Kilroy said she found the strength to go on. But each time she opened to a biblical passage she got the same message. She kept reading that nothing is impossible with God. She believed that if she just kept asking in Jesus' name, Mark would be returned to her.

March 26 would be Easter Sunday. That had always been a joyous family day for the Kilroys. Now, as Easter Sunday got closer with no sign of Mark, the date took on a deeply distressing symbolic significance for the Kilroy family.

"Mark has always come home for Easter," Helen told reporters.

On Friday, March 24, two days before Easter, Bradley Moore, Brent Martin, and Bill Huddleston again relived the last night they had seen Mark. This time it was as performers in front of the cameras of the Fox television network show "America's Most Wanted." The producers of the show had decided to film a five-minute segment, which would be seen nationally on Easter night. (Ironically, the show was not seen in the Rio

Grande Valley, where Mark was most likely to be found.)

The process of filming the show was, to say the least, taxing. Moore, Martin, and Huddleston played themselves, and actor Todd Roberts played Mark Kilroy. The boys had to go back in time, laugh, drink, and dance just as they had on that fateful night. The boys did their best, but the filming took its toll.

"Don't get me wrong," said an emotional Bradley Moore to one of the film crew when they got to the spot where Mark had vanished. "I'm not mad at you. But we've been having fun all night, and now this is the point where we lost him."

Easter came and went without Mark, and that perhaps more than anything else seemed to yank hope out from under the family. More and more the Kilroys were beginning to face the unthinkable.

"I feel he is going to come back to us," Helen Kilroy said to reporters. "Whoever has him, I just don't want them to be so frightened that they would fatally hurt Mark. We don't have any anger toward that person; we just want Mark back. With everyone praying like this, I don't see how the Lord can refuse us. But if Mark is taken from us, we have the hope of eternal life. He'll be alive forever. People who don't have that belief, I don't know how they could handle something like this."

The Kilroys clung to their religion throughout, perhaps never imagining that it was someone else's less benign religious beliefs that had taken their son from them.

On Sunday, April 2, Jim Kilroy went home,

along with his wife, who by that time had given up her place by the phone and gone to Brownsville. The sheriff's office had received more than two thousand phone calls on the case, many of them generated by the "America's Most Wanted" show. Nonetheless, the search, Oran Neck told Jim and Helen Kilroy, was at "absolute zero." The Kilroys planned to come back a week later and hand out more posters.

In Santa Fe, Texas, the people were with the Kilroys. Several events were planned to raise reward money. Jack Long, the mayor of Santa Fe, declared that April 12–16 would be Yellow Ribbon Days, during which Santa Fe residents would wear yellow ribbons to remind the public that the search for Mark went on. Santa Fe school kids wrote letters urging government officials to dedicate more resources to the investigation.

On Monday, April 10, San Antonio mayor Henry Cisneros lent his support to the case. Cisneros is a much-respected Mexican-American who has since left office and gone into private industry. Cisneros, whom Neck describes as "a gentleman and a half," held a news conference in Brownsville along with the mayors of Brownsville and Matamoros.

"Amidst a crowded street, a young man very suddenly disappeared," Cisneros said. "Somewhere there must be someone who saw something that might lead to the resolution of this case."

Later Cisneros told reporters, "I have no presumptions about what one more appeal can do. I do know these are very good people who have been dealt a bad hand."

But unknown to Cisneros, events in Mexico were leading to a tragic end to the search for Mark Kilroy. Just hours before Cisneros spoke, Juan Benitez had shown a picture of Mark Kilroy to the caretaker of a remote ranch outside of Matamoros.

"Have you seen this boy?" Benitez had asked.

"Yes," the caretaker had said.

THREE

The Discovery

As he drove west along Mexican Federal Highway 2 on the afternoon of Sunday, April 9, in a silver-colored Chevrolet, Serafin Hernandez Garcia thought he was invisible.

Serafin was returning from Brownsville, where he had gone to tell Adolfo Constanzo that a big drug delivery had been made. Serafin thought the police could not see him, because Adolfo Constanzo had told him they couldn't. Constanzo was El Padrino, the Godfather, and Serafin believed that El Padrino was always right.

"The police will not see you, and their bullets will bounce off you," El Padrino perhaps told him after performing the appropriate ebbo, a Santerian magic spell.

Perhaps it had occurred to Serafin, who was twenty, that if the police could not see him, there would be no need for their bullets to bounce off him. Perhaps not.

Perhaps, also, the belief that he was invisible

came easily to him not just because he seems to have been psychologically enslaved by Constanzo and drawn into a religion that allowed for such things. Maybe he also had been drinking Aguardiente Canoas, a cheap sugar-cane liquor that had just been outlawed in Mexico because it was known to cause hallucinations. The liquor was later found on the Santa Elena ranch where Serafin has admitted he helped keep watch over shipments of marijuana.

Whatever the reasons, young Serafin had faith in El Padrino's spells. He had seen them work. Ever since he had come under the influence of Constanzo, his grades at Texas Southmost College in Brownsville, where he was studying to be a police officer, had improved. And ever since Constanzo had taken control of the Hernandez family's drug gang, business had improved, and there had been no hassles with the police.

Serafin liked having money in his pocket. He liked having a telephone in his car. He liked the guns. He liked the way he and his friends could swagger about town, bragging about how they had the Mexican police in their pocket. And he liked being invisible.

But even though he liked the life of luxury that he had latched on to, there were times when he was filled with anxiety over the methods used to attain that life. The magic shield that El Padrino had put over the entire dope-smuggling operation had not come easily. Many had been murdered. Constanzo, it seemed, could snuff out a human life as easily as he could spit. And Serafin was afraid that if he made one mistake, said one wrong word, did one thing to displease El Padrino, his own head could come under Constanzo's machete, as others' had.

Serafin, an American citizen, thought that he would soon finish college and he would then get out, escape from the control of El Padrino. He would get a job as a cop in Brownsville. A strange choice for a young man who is described by fellow TSC students as a rebellious braggart who claimed to have the Matamoros police in his back pocket.

Serafin had changed a lot in two years. Back in 1986, when Mark Kilroy and Bill Huddleston were playing baseball at Santa Fe High School, Serafin was also playing baseball, thirty miles away at Nimitz High School in Houston. He was a handsome, athletic-looking, baby-faced young man who always dressed neatly and always looked, says one acquaintance, "freshly scrubbed."

Serafin had been born in Texas. He was an American citizen from a Mexican family and he lived comfortably in both cultures. Serafin dreamed of playing big-league baseball, though in fact he never really excelled at that sport, and by senior year he had become the team manager.

As a teen, Serafin lived in a middle-class area south of Houston, and the school he went to was mostly Anglos, with a smattering of Mexicans, Indians, and blacks. He visited Mexico often and must have thought how lucky he was to live in the U.S.A. In Mexico, it seemed, people worked hard but they ended up with a lot less. Many of them lived in squalor, and almost all of them lived in smaller quarters than his American friends. They lived for the most part without color TV sets, without phones. They drove older cars, or none at all. It probably seemed to Serafin that the Mexicans grew old faster and the lines of life's disappointments were etched more deeply on their faces than on the faces of Americans. He sure as hell didn't want to live that way.

He didn't have to.

Serafin had been born into a large, lower-class family that had many close branches in Matamoros. The generations before him had been impoverished farmers who for years had struggled to wring a meager living out of the sometimes stingy soil. But around the time that little Serafin was picking up his first plastic bat to knock a pinky ball across the front yard, his uncle Saul made a decision that would drastically alter the family fortunes and change the course of Serafin's life.

In the early 1970s, Saul announced to his brothers that he had decided to plow under his crops and grow something more lucrative: marijuana. Uncle Saul bought marijuana fields in Oaxaca and Yucatan, states in southern Mexico. He began trucking marijuana north. He stored it at remote ranches on both sides of the Rio Grande, including Rancho Santa Elena, which was owned by Serafin's grandfather, Elio Brigido Hernandez. Saul set up a distribution network in Houston, and he put his brother, Serafin's father, whose name is Serafin Hernandez Rivera, in charge. Eventually Saul brought two more of his brothers, Ovidio and Elio, into the family business. Though Ovidio and Elio were uncles to Serafin, they were close to his own age. At twenty-eight, Ovidio was eight years older than Serafin, and Elio was only three years older than his nephew.

Even at an early age, Serafin could see the change in his uncles. They started wearing expensive suits, driving luxurious cars. They ate at fine restaurants, they tipped big. They had, it seemed, purchased respectability.

"The Hernandez family has got cash and pull," a family friend once said. "A person messes with the Hernandez family and he doesn't live to see another day. There are millions of people in the world. One or two less doesn't mean much to them."

While young Serafin was still in high school, he was invited to join the family business. His job, police now believe, was to smuggle marijuana from storage areas in Matamoros over the border and up to Houston.

Things were going well for Serafin. He wore fancy jewelry. He had money in his designer jeans; he had friends in school; he had baseball.

Still, back then it seemed to everyone that Serafin was a nice enough kid. If he was taking drugs at all, it was never evident in his grades or in his behavior at school. Friends say he was compassionate. Once, when he was involved in an auto accident, he ran a mile to get help for his injured friend. He was a kid who wanted nice things, but there is no indication that back then he planned to acquire them through a life of crime. Quite the opposite. His dream, besides that of becoming a major leaguer, even then was to become a cop.

When Serafin graduated from high school in

1986, he wrote in his yearbook that he wanted to go to college and play baseball. By this time, though, he had already embarked on the path of crime, though he probably didn't see it that way.

And he probably didn't feel like a criminal. He still wanted to be a police officer and catch bad guys. He probably thought he would smuggle marijuana just until he had a good job.

But in 1987 the whole operation damn near fell apart, and Serafin was pulled more deeply into the family business.

The disaster that struck the Hernandez family came indirectly as a result of what was perhaps the most publicized Mexican drug-related murder before 1989. On February 1, 1985, U.S. Drug Enforcement Administration agent Enrique Camarena was kidnapped and murdered in Guadalajara. The Mexican police eventually arrested Tomás Morlet, a twenty-two-year veteran of the Mexican federal police. Morlet was alleged to be the mastermind behind the kidnapping and shooting. However, the DEA didn't think that Morlet was the leader of the gang responsible for Camarena's murder, so Morlet was set free, apparently in hopes that he would lead lawmen to bigger fish.

It seems that Morlet had become a serious liability for somebody, and one night in January of 1987 he came out of a nightclub in Matamoros and was met by a man with a machine gun, who shot him dead. The man who had the misfortune of being Morlet's dinner companion that night was Saul Hernandez, and he, too, was murdered by the assassin.

The death of Saul Hernandez, like the death of any legitimate CEO, had a chilling effect on the business.

"What are we going to do?" Serafin's father probably asked. "Who the hell do we pay off?"

Elio and Ovidio, too, were shaken by Saul's death. It had always been Saul who had the final word, who took care of things, and now they were left alone and it felt as if they were losing their grip on the marijuana business they had worked so hard to build up.

"Tell me," Serafin senior must have said, "who the hell are we supposed to pay off?" He perhaps threw his hands in the air, while the other brothers shook their heads.

"You know," Elio might have said, "someone could take this all away from us."

"Who? What are you talking about?"

"The big guys in Mexico," Elio would say. "They bribe everybody, government officials. Nobody could touch them. They could come here and put us out of business."

Serafin perhaps listened quietly as the uncles considered their position. Saul, they complained, had not kept them up to speed on the business. They didn't know all the levers of power they had to pull. They didn't know all the contacts or how exactly to get money.

"And what about the police?" Ovidio might have asked. "You think they're going to let us work if the money stops coming in? They can get their bribes from someone else."

There were many such meetings. There was a lot of handwringing, and in time a lot of finger pointing. Everytime a shipment wasn't made or a payment wasn't received, one brother would blame the other.

"Saul was very powerful," says Matamoros police commandant Juan Benitez, "and when he was around they were all together, driving great cars and making money. After he died they didn't have the contacts Saul had. They didn't know where the money would come from, and they started to have serious problems. There was a division."

Family loyalty was being stretched to the limit. To young Serafin it must have sometimes seemed that his family was like the gang that couldn't shoot straight. Somehow the Hernandez family muddled through, but profits plummeted and the family's sphere of influence seemed to shrink daily.

On February 4, 1987, Serafin Hernandez Rivera was arrested at a secret Texas airstrip where some of his associates were trying to land a planeload of marijuana. He and eight other men were charged with conspiring to import marijuana. He was freed on $25,000 bond and as of August 1989 has not been tried for the crime.

According to Grimes County District Attorney David Barron, Serafin Hernandez Rivera was set free so that he could lead authorities to "other suspects higher up on the ladder."

Perhaps this plane fiasco made more urgent the gang's need for a top dog. In any case, it was around this time that the battle for leadership began. Elio in Mexico and Serafin senior in Houston both wanted to run the show. Before long the cousins and the in-laws were choosing sides. Young Serafin took a good hard look at the situation and eventually threw in his hand with his young uncle, Elio, not his father, for reasons that have never been made clear. Ovidio also got behind Elio. If the two sides agreed on one thing, it was that the family business was falling apart, and that if they didn't settle their differences soon, there would be nothing left to fight over.

In August of 1988 the family skirmish took on the dimension of a soap opera when Serafin and Elio showed up at the Cameron County sheriff's office to report that Ovidio and Ovidio's two-year-old son had been kidnapped by a Hernandez cousin, Jesús (Jesse) Maria Hernandez, an ally of Serafin the elder, who lived in Brownsville.

"They were crying like babies to save their nephew," says Cameron County Deputy Sheriff George Gavito.

Elio and Serafin told police that an $800,000 ransom had been demanded and that the kidnappers had threatened to kill Ovidio and his son. But a day later Elio and Serafin informed police that Ovidio and his son had been released and that the whole thing was a family matter that would be settled by the family. Nobody is quite sure of what exactly happened, but police believe the whole matter is connected to a dope deal gone bad in which Elio and Serafin either stole the $800,000 from their own family, or had it stolen from them, and that Jesse had kidnapped the Ovidios at the Amigo shopping mall in Brownsville to try to get it back.

In any case, this fiasco was just one more demonstration of the fact that the Hernandez brothers had, in the words of Juan Benitez, "lost faith in each other," and it seemed they needed some sort of outside protection. Their destiny was moving inexorably toward a link with a man named Adolfo de Jesús Constanzo.

There is no universally accepted story about how Elio Hernandez first met Adolfo Constanzo, the mysterious Cuban American who would lead the Hernandez family to ruin.

In one version, told in several newspaper stories, the Hernandez gang went to Constanzo, whom they had heard about from Alvaro de Leon, also known as El Duby, who was a friend of Elio's and also a member of Constanzo's Mexico City following.

There is a small bar near the downtown market district of Brownsville, where, allegedly, Elio and his friends sometimes drank. Possibly Elio sat down with his friend El Duby in the bar at a small square table, with the ceiling fan whirling above his head, and bought drinks. He might have told El Duby about the family, and in time talk could have turned to the family's business problems. He would recount all the woes the family had experienced since the death of Saul.

"We just feel, I don't know . . . desperate, all the time," he would say to his friend. "Look, we're not big-time smugglers. We're just trying to run our business and not bother anybody. But there are big guys out there. And they have friends in high places and we don't. And we feel vulnerable, you know, vulnerable."

El Duby would lean back in his wooden chair. "You need the Cuban," he must have said.

"The Cuban?"

"Adolfo Constanzo," the young man would explain. "He can protect you."

"Protect us? How?"

El Duby must have smiled. "Lots of ways. He has many friends in high places. Police. Government officials. He knows who to take care of and who not to. He is an extremely persuasive man."

"How old is he?"

"Twenty-five."

"Young, like us."

"Yes, but he knows the ways of the world. He can protect you. It will cost, but he can do it."

Perhaps El Duby implied that Constanzo had powers that went beyond the buying of influence and the use of violence. Constanzo was a Cuban American from Miami who had gotten a reputation as a charismatic and sometimes frightening figure who moved like a shadow through the world of Mexico City's gay bars in the Zona Rosa, the "pink zone."

In other stories, however, it is Constanzo who sought out Elio. And the friend who connects them is not El Duby, but Sara Aldrete. Oran Neck is convinced that Sara Aldrete, the Texas Southmost College student who would later become known as the Witch, introduced the men. Juan Benitez agrees.

"From the interrogation that we conducted, we learned that Sara Aldrete had a connection to all this, to Constanzo, through her boyfriend Elio. Elio had been Sara's boyfriend, Sara knew Elio was a drug dealer. Constanzo asked Sara to tell him if she had any friends in the Mafia so he could gain protection through the Mafia.

"Sara introduces Constanzo to Elio, who in turn introduces Serafin and David [Serna] and Sergio [Martinez], which was the band that Elio brought with him. And they start trafficking."

It seems likely that this is the correct story, that Sara introduced Constanzo to Elio, whom she had known for years. They had been sweethearts at age fourteen, and after Sara was married at age nineteen and divorced eight months later, she and Elio took up again, though, she says, just as friends.

In any case, what we do know for certain is that Elio and Constanzo met early in 1988, and some sort of deal was struck.

Constanzo apparently became the supplier of some drugs. "But he was never the main supplier," Oran Neck says. More importantly, Constanzo's job, it seems, was to arrange for payoffs to high-ranking Mexican officials. He would make certain that the Hernandez marijuana-smuggling business proceeded smoothly.

"Constanzo was never his own boss," George Gavito says. "He always answered to someone higher in a larger Mexican marijuana ring."

Gavito, it should be noted, is talking about Constanzo's drug-smuggling activities. The ritual murders, for which Constanzo would become infamous, have never been connected to anyone higher, anonymous or otherwise.

In return for his influence Constanzo was brought into the Hernandez family business and given, Mexican police believe, 50 percent of the profits. The figure sounds high, but we have no way of knowing how many people Constanzo had to bribe from his share. It was a deal that would bring profit to everybody for a while. But it was, in a more than figurative sense, a deal that was made with the devil. Though Constanzo started out as a middleman, he was a powerful personality who inspired devotion, and long before April 9, 1989, he had become the boss of the Hernandez drug-smuggling ring.

Now, as Serafin Hernandez García guided the silver Chevy along Highway 2 on his return from Brownsville, he worried that if he didn't get out of the family business soon, the devil would get him. But it was too late. Juan Benitez was about to get him, instead.

Benitez, thirty-five, is a good-looking young man, with long, dark hair and strong features that reveal his Indian heritage. He has a soft, vulnerable look about him that had inspired Gary Cartwright, writing in *Texas Monthly,* to describe him as having "Bambi eyes." Cartwright also notes that Benitez "usually wore jeans and a Philadelphia Eagles football jacket," which has become his trademark. But there is nothing frivolous about him. He is a man, says Tony Zavaleta, the anthropology professor at Texas Southmost College, who is "stern, serious, professional, courteous, but very much in control."

From his small and cluttered office on the first floor of the Federal Judicial Police headquarters, Benitez had commanded the Matamoros garrison since February 1989. It was not a job coveted among Mexican lawmen; by many it was regarded as a dead end, a path that veered from the mainstream of advancement. But Benitez had brought substance, as well as style, to the job. He had swept into Matamoros like a fresh breeze and had begun to earn back respect for a job whose previous occupant had allegedly socked away millions of dollars in bribe money and confiscated property. Benitez had made more drug arrests than any of his predecessors. And now, he was about to break up the Hernandez gang.

Juan Benitez had heard talk about Rancho Santa Elena for some time. There had been rumors that the ranch was a holding zone for large, U.S.-bound shipments of marijuana. There were other rumors, more sketchy, of satanic activities on the ranch. Black magic was done there, it was said; people had been murdered.

Juan Benitez was about to find out it was all true.

The events that led directly to the arrest of Serafin Hernandez and three other members of the gang, and later to the discovery of dismembered bodies, have been reported in a variety of ways. Juan Benitez himself describes the events leading up to the arrests most clearly:

"Serafin Hernandez passed through a checkpoint

on the third of April. [On April 1, Mexican anti-drug-smuggling units had begun stopping cars along the U.S.-Mexican border. This was part of a tough offensive ordered by the new Mexican president, Carlos Salinas de Gortari, and implemented by the Federal Judicial Police, the army, the federal highway police, and planes and helicopters. This joint U.S.-Mexican operation was, according to a spokesman for the Mexican attorney general's office, "possibly the largest of its kind."] On April third, we followed him to the ranch at a safe distance, so as not to be noticed. We left somebody to watch the ranch. Two days later we went back to the ranch. We talked to Domingo Reyes, the caretaker. He told us the ranch belonged to the Hernandez family, which was being investigated for dealing in narcotics. On April fifth, we found that they had hidden marijuana in a small storehouse on the ranch, but we didn't arrest anybody that day. We put the ranch under surveillance to see who would show up.

"Domingo went and told the Hernandezes that we had been there, so they stopped going to the ranch. But on Saturday, April eighth, we discovered that they had sneaked in during the night and removed all but fifty kilos of the marijuana and made a delivery with it.

"On Sunday morning, the ninth of April, Serafin drove to Brownsville to tell Constanzo that the drugs had been delivered. It was when he was on his way back that we arrested him. Then we arrested Elio Hernandez, David Serna, and Sergio Martinez. The only one who resisted was Sergio.

He was violent. But none of them had weapons when we arrested them. We found weapons later at their homes.

"We didn't know that the deaths were occurring. We were just investigating for narcotics. Once we had the men detained in an interrogation room, that's when we began to suspect that they had kidnapped Kilroy, and late that Sunday I went back to the ranch and showed the photo of Kilroy to Domingo Reyes."

To get to the Santa Elena ranch from Matamoros, Benitez had to drive out of town on Highway 2 toward Reynosa. Like most highways in Mexico, this one was narrow and in need of repairs. About fifteen miles out of town he came to a big curve, known as the Texas curve. Just beyond was the entrance to the ranch.

"Ranch" is a word that loses much in the translation. Around Matamoros it used to differentiate the property from *ejidos* or collective farms. People who work on the *ejidos* live on the *ejidos,* but ranch owners, if they can afford it, live in town.

Benitez drove down the narrow road that led onto the property through a cornfield. After a mile or so, when he was two fields deep from the highway, he came to a barn where farm equipment was kept, the same barn where Mark Kilroy had been held the night he was kidnapped. Benitez continued on to the small, ramshackle house where Domingo Reyes lived. Beyond that, to the right, was the shack where the rituals were held. There were woods on one side of the shack and on the other side hay was piled up to prevent anyone at the ranch house from seeing in. Near the shack was a corral, a fenced-in area where cattle were sometimes kept. Santa Elena, he could see, was a working farm, with a crop of corn, cattle, goats, and other livestock.

On Sunday evening when Benitez showed the picture of Mark Kilroy to Domingo Reyes and asked him if he recognized the boy, Domingo said, "Yes."

Reyes went on in matter-of-fact tones, "I remember, I gave him a drink of water. Later they took him down to the shack, and after that I never saw him anymore."

The federales, with Domingo in tow, drove over to the shack, passing through a barbed wire fence to reach it. The windows were shuttered, the doors were padlocked, and there was a foul stench coming from inside. The federales, suspecting that there was a corpse inside, broke the locks.

There wasn't much to the fifteen-by-twenty-five-foot shack—four walls, two doors, and a couple of windows that were boarded up.

The first officer inside, a man known as "The Tiger," came out quickly, vomiting. What had sickened him was three pots of rancid stew, one of which contained a cooked human brain.

The federales gave the shack time to air out, then Benitez went inside. Slowly his eyes adjusted to the darkness and shadows in the shack. What he saw disturbed him.

A big iron cauldron stood near the middle of the room. In it there was dried blood, parts of a human brain, and a roasted turtle. In another smaller kettle there was human hair, a goat's head, more blood, and parts of a chicken. Scattered around the area were melted candles, half-burned cigars, garlic. Benitez may not have recognized everything he was seeing at the time, but he knew that what he was seeing was part of something wicked.

"Brujería!" he called to the others. Witchcraft.

FOUR

The Digging

Benitez arrested four members of the Hernandez gang on April 9:

Elio Hernandez Rivera, twenty-three. Elio was born in Brownsville, Texas, and he lived in Matamoros. He is married, and the father of a two-year-old boy.

Serafin Hernandez Garcia, twenty. Serafin, Elio's nephew, lived in Brownsville at the time of the arrests.

David Serna Martinez, twenty-two. David was a student at Tamaulipas State University in Ciudad Victoria. (Matamoros is in the state of Tamaulipas.) He was born in Matamoros.

Sergio Martinez Solis, twenty-three. Sergio, cousin to David, was born in Mexico and lived in Weslaco, Texas.

Domingo Reyes, twenty-seven, was also taken into custody as a material witness and was later charged with withholding information.

After long hours of questioning on the night of

Sunday, April 9, the prisoners began to confirm Benitez's darkest suspicions.

They confessed to kidnapping Mark Kilroy and described his murder. But there was more, much more. At first reluctantly, and then with repugnant cockiness, they told tales of unimaginable horror. They had fallen, it seemed, under the black wings of a modern-day Dracula, a prince of darkness. His name was Adolfo de Jesús Constanzo, but throughout they called him simply El Padrino.

Their stories were not just those of a ruthless drug gang protecting its business. The killing went far beyond that. It was satanic. They told tales of murder and mutilation and voodoo. There were bodies, they said, lots of them. Constanzo was a Santerian priest, they said. At other points in the conversations, though, he was a mayombero or tata nkisis, a black witch of Palo Mayombe, a man of great powers, a man who cannot be punished by the law. At still other times, he was the devil himself.

It must have seemed to Benitez that these young men had a tenuous understanding of the religion that held them in its grip. The amalgam of Afro-Caribbean beliefs could be the delusions of a madman, or the carefully calculated invention of a clever manipulator. In any case, as Benitez listened to his prisoners, it sometimes seemed to be something that Constanzo had made up as he went along. The culprits told Benitez about other members of the cult, all male, except for Sara Aldrete.

Sara, a twenty-four-year-old honors student at Texas Southmost College in Brownsville, was, they said, the *madrina*, Constanzo's aide. She was a beauty, they said, over six feet tall and able to lure men to her side.

The exact circumstances of the questioning and the original confessions can only be guessed at. Some lawmen in Texas hint that physical abuse might have been used to encourage the confessions. George Gavito, for example, says, "Confessing in Mexico is not the same as confessing in the U.S." Gary Cartwright, reporting in *Texas Monthly,* writes, "When a reporter asked how the federales had gotten confessions so quickly, Gavito pointed to a bottle of mineral water—federales like to shake the bottle and squirt water up the noses of reluctant witnesses."

More frightening, perhaps, than the tales the young prisoners told was the tone they took. They talked about the murders the way you might talk about the dinner you'd eaten or a movie you had seen. They even laughed at times as they described the killings.

"What about the American?" Benitez asked.

"Yes, he is there," Elio Hernandez told him.

"With the others?"

"Yes, with the others."

"How do you know?"

"I buried him," Elio said.

Of all the stories the young men told, perhaps the most apalling concerned their youngest victim. It was a tale they began by telling Benitez about one of the men they had killed.

"Somehow he had concealed a gun," Elio said. "He pulled a pistol on us, so I had to shoot him before we could have a ceremony."

"And what did you do then?" Benitez asked.

"We had to get another sacrifice," one of the others said.

"And?"

"So we went out and grabbed the first person we saw. We didn't know who it was, just some kid looking for his goat. We threw a bag over his head; we brought him back."

"And then what happened?"

"Elio, he cut the boy's head off with the machete. Then when we buried him we saw."

"Saw what?"

"It was José."

"Who is José?" Benitez asked.

"Elio's cousin," he was told.

"I see," Benitez said.

After the initial interrogation, Juan Benitez told Lieutenant Gavito that there was reason to think that Mark Kilroy's body would be found at the Santa Elena ranch.

Gavito called the Kilroys.

"I think by this time they had accepted the fact that Mark was dead," Gwen Huddleston says. "It had been a long time. They had just come back from another Brownsville trip; they had gone down to hand out more posters. And that trip had been extended because a body had been found up in northern Mexico, and the police at first thought it might be Mark."

Mrs. Huddleston was at the Kilroys' house the following evening when the phone rang. The Kilroys were being filmed for the "Inside Edition" television show. Gwen took the call in their bedroom. It was George Gavito asking for Mark's dental records.

"It was like six or seven in the evening and I had to rush around like crazy to get to the dentist's office and then to the airport to send the records to Brownsville. They had an officer waiting at the airport in Brownsville to hand-deliver them."

Even though Benitez knew about the bodies by late Sunday or early Monday, digging did not begin until Tuesday. In fact, U.S. lawmen say it was not until Tuesday at one A.M. that the Mexicans informed the Americans about the Sunday-night confessions.

After Benitez saw what was in the shack on Sunday, the investigation came to a temporary halt. He knew that he was about to uncover unspeakable crimes, and he knew what he had to do. On Monday, he hired a *curandero,* a healer, to do a sweep of the area around the shack at Rancho Santa Elena.

Anthony Zavaleta, who specializes in *curandismo* (the local border folk religions), explains:

"When it became obvious to the commandant what this was, they brought the *curandero,* the healer, in to perform what we call a *limpia,* a ritual blessing or cleansing of the area. By calling in the *curandero* Benitez was doing the appropriate thing for his culture. I would have done the same thing. In Mexico this is very typical."

Zavaleta points out that this cleansing to rid the area of evil spirits was not just a symbolic gesture to keep the populace happy.

"There is no question that Benitez believes in

81

this," Zavaleta says. "I believe in it, and I've got a Ph.D. in anthropology."

This is all part of what Zavaleta calls "folk Catholicism."

"You can be a Catholic and still believe all of these things," he says. "Just as Santeria in the Caribbean is folk Catholicism, *curandismo* is folk Catholicism in this border region of Mexico. It is a strange mixture of pagan beliefs and Catholicism. Not modern Catholicism the way you and I might know it, but a folk Catholicism, almost a medieval kind of thing, very steeped in magic and superstition and ritual."

Though Zavaleta was not at this *limpia,* he says there are certain culturally appropriate things that the *curandero* probably did.

"He would have more than likely sprinkled some type of holy water, which would probably have come from a church or shrine. He would have brought some sort of oil and probably herbs. Sweeps are often done with a sprig of basil. He would have gone around the property, particularly the area of the shack, making incantations and prayers to cast out the devil."

On Tuesday morning, April 11, Juan Benitez, along with George Gavito, led a small army of Mexican police onto the ranch, along with the handcuffed prisoners.

Sergio Martinez told the police where he thought Kilroy's body was buried. The police brought in a ditch-digging machine and a field hand to operate it. They found two bodies, one cut open with the heart apparently removed. Neither body was

Kilroy's. Sergio apologized. Serafin told Benitez that he knew where the body was.

"Show me where the American is buried," Benitez said.

Serafin led him to the spot just outside the rickety wooden corral.

The grave was not hard to find. As Cartwright explains in his *Texas Monthly* piece, "Serafin told investigators that he had buried Kilroy, and he led the way to Kilroy's grave, which was marked by a piece of wire sticking out of the ground. The other end of the wire had been attached to Kilroy's spinal column so that when his body decomposed members of the cult could pull out the vertebrae to make into a necklace."

Benitez handed young Serafin a shovel. "Dig," he said.

Twenty minutes later when Serafin finished tossing away the dirt that had covered Mark Kilroy, Benitez looked down into the grave. Kilroy's brain and heart had been cut out, just as the young men had said. Then it was true, he must have thought, they had not made up this horror, they had not exaggerated. Examining the dark, moist soil to try to sort out what was part of the mutilated body and what was not, he realized that Kilroy's legs had been chopped off above the knees.

"Was that part of your ritual?" he asked.

"No," Serafin told him without emotion. "It just made him easier to bury."

It was ten A.M. on April 11 when they finished uncovering the body of Mark Kilroy.

Throughout the day more bodies were dug up.

Hearses and body bags were brought in from area funeral homes. Brownsville area reporters came in by helicopter. They set up a tent, ate sandwiches, drank Coke.

In all Benitez and his men found twelve bodies buried in eight graves that day. The victims had been tortured. They had been mutilated. Hearts and brains and lungs had been removed. Genitals had been ripped off. In time the details of many of the murders would be known around the world.

Early on the morning of Wednesday, April 12, the American lawmen held a press conference in front of the Brownsville courthouse. They announced to the world that the bodies of Mark Kilroy and eleven others had been found. Later that day in Matamoros another press conference was held. At this one the prisoners were paraded out to tell the world about their crimes. (See Chapter Seven.)

On Thursday, April 13, the body count rose to thirteen when Juan Benitez went back to Rancho Santa Elena, this time with the prisoner Sergio Martinez in tow. In their wake were dozens of reporters covering this story, which was breaking like a wave over the Western Hemisphere and much of the rest of the world. Martinez had told Benitez about a body that was not yet accounted for.

Martinez, who was known as "the butterfly" (according to Sara Aldrete, Constanzo gave homosexual nicknames to several of his friends), walked across the corral to a spot just outside the fence. "Here," he said.

"Give him a shovel and pick," Benitez said to one of his federales. An officer turned over the tools to Martinez.

"Dig," Benitez said.

It was a hot morning. It had been raining off and on for days, and now the stench left behind by the decaying bodies hung like a gaseous cloud in the still and humid air. Several of the reporters and soldiers wore surgical face masks to keep from gagging. Even as Martinez dug, questions were shouted.

"I didn't kill anyone," he said. "I helped kidnap them, that's all, and I buried them. I didn't actually kill anyone."

Benitez perhaps thought about this man Constanzo as he listened to the metallic sound of the shovel in the background. Who was this monster? Where would he go, what would he do? He'll get no protection in Mexico, that's for sure. Nobody will protect this man, not even the drug dealers. He is too hot. Perhaps he has gone to Miami. Or Houston. As he stood by the gravesite, perhaps the commandant tried to chart in his mind the motives and movements of this bizarre villain.

If Benitez's thoughts did drift, there was a sudden reminder of where he was when a new and more potent stench filled his nostrils. It was as if somebody had suddenly punctured a sewer pipe. Reporters who didn't have masks gagged, as did Martinez, down in his hole, surrounded by machine-gun-toting soldiers. He had begun to uncover the body.

"Dig," Benitez said.

A cameraman pulled off his surgical mask and handed it to Martinez. The prisoner went back to work, shoveling the last layers of dirt until the remains were visible.

The body that Martinez uncovered was that of a man, thirty years old or so. The man had been blindfolded and gagged. His heart had been ripped out. His genitals had been sliced off. A rope was tied around the feet of the corpse and Martinez tugged on it until the body was free.

Benitez ordered Martinez out of the hole. Maybe it seemed to him somehow wrong to let Martinez help with the removal of the body. Maybe it seemed wrong to let him touch this poor soul again. Some of Benitez's men climbed down into the hole and lifted the remains out, while Martinez calmly leaned on the corral fence and answered reporters' questions.

On the following Sunday, April 16, the body count rose to a final fifteen when Hidalgo Castillo Vasquez, seventy-seven, told police he had reason to believe a body, possibly that of his son, was buried in an orchard not far from the Santa Elena ranch. Mr. Castillo led federales to the orchard, where they dug up the body of Mr. Vasquez's fifty-two-year-old son and another man. The bodies had not been mutilated. Police believe that the men were killed after they witnessed a truckload of marijuana being unloaded.

Juan Benitez told reporters that the orchard was part of a ranch co-owned by Elio Hernandez Rivera.

Mr. Castillo explained that he thought the body might be there because shortly after his son disappeared some children said they had seen people burying a body in the orchard. But that was long before the discovery at Santa Elena, and he had dismissed it as a child's imaginative tale.

FIVE

The Religion

When Adolfo Constanzo died in a hail of machine gun bullets, he took with him the answers to those questions that haunt us whenever we hear that a Constanzo, or a Jim Jones, or even an Adolf Hitler, has bitten the dust. What on earth does it feel like to be so unredeemably evil? Was it really true, could Constanzo just slice a machete into the head of a Mark Kilroy as easily as you and I slap a mosquito? Did he feel nothing at all when he took a human life?

In the short time since his death, Constanzo's reputation for wickedness has swollen to mythical proportions, and most of the people who knew him are, understandably, not enthusiastic about discussing him with a journalist. Some of his associates do not want the notoriety that comes with being linked in print to so poisonous a personality. Others are less abstract in their concern. Simply put, they don't want to die. In their mind there lingers the fear that El Padrino will bound up from his grave and punish them for their indiscretion. So there is much about the man that will never be known, and much that might never be told. But from the memories of those people who do talk about Constanzo, and from the centuries-old traditions of the curious religion that he practiced, a religion that is a way of life, we can surmise a good deal about him.

Adolfo de Jesús Constanzo grew up in a poor Cuban American family in one of those boringly flat and tropical Dade County neighborhoods that stretch west from Miami, where the small one-storied houses are lined up like pretty clay boxes, and the highest fronds of the palm trees have turned brown from the sun.

His mother is variously known as Delia Aurora Gonzalez del Valle, Aurora Gonzalez Constanzo, and Delia Posada. We will call her Aurora Constanzo. After the gruesome discovery in Matamoros, Aurora would say that she was "shocked and scared" by the allegations about her son. "I brought him up," she would say. "I held him in my arms. I can't believe someone would be like that, that he could change so abruptly."

But according to the neighbors in the tight little community around Southwest Ninety-fourth Court, where Constanzo spent his teenage years, Adolfo was one nut that didn't fall too far from the tree. His mother, they imply, was a bit difficult to get along with. "She was," says one neighbor, whispering softly, "a witch. And that's why none of the kids would play with little Adolfo."

The neighbors say that if you got on the wrong

side of Aurora Constanzo, you stood a good chance of finding the headless corpse of a chicken or even a goat on your front step next to the *Miami Herald* in the morning. Galena Torres, whose family lived two doors from the Constanzos', says she once found the corpse of a goose out front, and she's convinced that Adolfo's mother put it there because of some dispute with the family. Others report that the streets were often littered with the discarded carcasses of animals that Aurora Constanzo had ritually sacrificed. One woman who later moved into the house where Constanzo had lived reports that the house had an altar, and the evidence of the ritualism was scattered all about. The neighbors say that Aurora was cruel and vindictive, that she would put curses on people.

Perhaps Adolfo's mother was just an eccentric. She has certainly not been accused of any major felonies, though in May 1989 she was sentenced to two years in jail for stealing a refrigerator. In any case, it cannot be denied that Aurora was an imposing and influential figure who cast a very large shadow on the life of young Constanzo. His last words, before he ordered his own execution, were, "This is it, Mother."

Constanzo's mother allegedly practiced a relatively benign religion called Santeria, and a more aggressive religion with similar roots, Palo Mayombe.

Despite whatever other emotional scarring might have helped to turn Adolfo into a sociopath, it is clear that religion played a part. In the amorality and magical systems of Santeria and the Palo

Mayombe religion, which he progressed to, we can see the seeds of the havoc that he would later wreak. That is not to say that these religions cause sociopathic behavior. But if we can assume that young Adolfo was a deeply disturbed person, we can also assume that he was deeply entranced by the ideas of magic contained in both religions and that from them he must have drawn the rationale for his fiendish behavior.

Santeria evolved in Cuba in the nineteenth century from the ancient African religion of Nigeria's Yoruban people, many of whom were enslaved and brought to Cuba to work on sugar plantations. Since they were forbidden to practice their African religion openly, they often pretended to worship the Catholic saints of their masters, but in fact were hiding their orishas, or gods, in the Catholic icons. Sometimes this took the form of stashing stones that represented their orishas under the statues of saints. In time, the hiding was forgotten and they simply began to identify their gods with the saints, thus creating Santeria, which literally means "the worship of saints." For example, the Yoruban god Changó becomes in Santeria the Catholic saint Barbara. Babalu-Ayé becomes Saint Lazarus. Oya becomes Our Lady of La Candelaria, and so forth. Similarly, many African symbols have been replaced by Catholic symbols.

The Yoruban pantheon was composed of fourteen orishas, born of the goddess Yemaya, and another fifteen gods from various sources. Like everything in Santeria, the pantheon is colorful and complex. There are talents, colors, messengers, and symbols associated with individual gods, and each god has a story and a very human set of personality traits.

The fourteen gods of Yemaya are:

Ayé-Shaluga, the god of good fortune, represented by a seashell.

Changó, the god of fire, thunder, and lightning. Changó lives in the clouds, from where he sends thunderbolts when an offering has been made to him. Changó likes to eat special foods and smoke cigars. (Likewise, a santero who has been possessed by Changó would do these things.)

Chankpana, the god of smallpox, is represented by an old man nursing a lacerated leg. His symbol is a red and white cane, and flies and mosquitoes are his messengers.

Dada, represented by a pumpkin, is the god of unborn children and gardens.

Oba, the goddess of the river, is the wife of Changó. She is jealous of Changó because he is a philanderer, and she is always following him around.

Ochosi, symbolized by a bow and arrow, is the god of birds, wild animals, and hunters.

Ochu is the goddess of the moon. (She is not a popular deity these days.)

Oke, the god of mountains, looks out for people who live in high places.

Olokun, a long-haired, hermaphrodite god, lives in the ocean with mermaids.

Olosa helps fishermen. Her messenger is the crocodile.

Orisha-Oko, the god of harvests. His messenger is the honeybee.

Oshún, the mistress of Changó, is the goddess of love and gold.

Orun, the god of the sun. Like the moon goddess, he is not called upon often.

Oyá, the patroness of justice, can help improve the memory.

The other orishas of Santeria are:

Aroni, the god of medicine.

Ayé, goddess of the jungle.

Babalu-Ayé, patron saint of the sick.

Bascoso, founder of the Yoruba dynasty.

Chiyidi, god of nightmares, used to torment enemies.

Elegguá, a particularly powerful god who opens and closes doors. He protects entrances to homes.

Ibeyi, twin god protectors of children.

Ifá, the god of impossible things and palm trees.

Ochumare, goddess of the rainbow.

Oggun, god of war and iron.

Olarosa, protector of homes.

Olimerin, protector of villages.

Orúnla, owner of the divination system.

Osachin, the patron of doctors.

Oyé, the giant god of storms.

The name of one of these gods has been heard hundreds of times by most Americans, though probably few realized they were hearing the name of a Yoruban deity. He is Babalu-Ayé, patron of the sick. Babalu-Ayé is represented by a leprous old man with two dogs, and his symbol is a pair of crutches. It was this god that you heard invoked in song many times by Cuban actor Desi Arnaz on "I Love Lucy."

Devotion to these orishas is vital to Santerian life. Santeros believe that everyone has a destiny in life and that each person is responsible for understanding his or her destiny and growing with it. It is the orishas who can bring the santero to the fulfillment of his destiny.

The santero can get occasional glimpses of this destiny through a complex process called divination. There is a lot more to divination than can be written here, but here is an example:

A santero has a problem. Let's say he's afraid that he will lose his job. He goes to a babalawo, a male who, by reason of extensive training, is the highest level of priest in the religion. The babalawo will throw a small chain, called an ekwele, that has eight pieces of shell and bone attached to it, and each piece of the chain can land in one of two ways, allowing for 256 different combinations. Each combination represents a life situation. The combination that falls will refer to some story from the Yoruban legends, and in the story the santero will see the solution to his problem. In addition, the priest may tell the santero to sacrifice a goat or drink a certain herbal tea. Any number of spiritual steps might be suggested.

More significantly, especially in the context of the Constanzo case, santeros believe that through divination the priest cannot only see solutions, but can, with magic, effect them. Just as Christians use prayer in an attempt to intervene in the natural flow of events, santeros use a complex form of magic, which is called sorcery by some and witch-craft or voodoo by others. The Spanish word is *brujería*. For the sake of simplicity we will call it magic. Furthermore, and this accounts in part for the hold Constanzo had over his followers, the believers in this and other African religions don't think that the priests' powers are limited to white magic. Black magic is also possible. In other words, the priest can create a spell that will bring you good luck, but he can also do a spell that will kill you.

Most Santerian spells, though, are not deadly. For example, let's say you would like to dominate someone, to overcome someone. This is what you would do: Wait until Tuesday. Then write the name of that person on a piece of paper. Then buy a spool of black thread, and that evening, as you go for a long walk, hold the piece of paper in one hand while with the other, you slowly wrap the thread around the paper. When the spool is empty, the paper is completely covered with the thread, and it is then that you throw the wrapped paper beneath a bush or a tree. Then you go home, taking a com-pletely different route.

If you have an enemy you would like to get rid of, a Santerian spell is to sprinkle powders made of garlic, cumin seed, salt, and some cigar ashes at your enemy's door. According to *Santeria: African Magic in Latin America,* "The person thus be-witched will not last long at that address."

The aspect of the orishas that is perhaps most controversial to outsiders is that they require sacri-fices in return for their good works. Each god has a favorite food, and often this requires the sacrifice of live animals, which is certainly the most widely known and most provocative aspect of Santeria, and one that has created a good deal of prejudice against the santeros.

Another dramatic aspect of Santeria, not well known to the general public, is ceremonial spirit mediumship. At some ceremonies an orisha will "seize the head" of a believer. The santero who is so possessed might do extraordinary dances and behave in uninhibited ways that would not be typical of him, and the god within him will deliver various messages, warnings, and advice to the gathering.

Here, referring to santeros by the names of the gods who have possessed them, is writer Enrique Fernandez talking about witnessing such possessions in *Tropic* magazine (March 13, 1988):

"Two or three times someone who had touched or had been touched by an orisha started to slip into a trance and had to be taken out of the room. At the rear the initiate, in a glittering blue gown, danced barefoot on the straw mat in front of her throne. Meanwhile the master of the revels, also barefoot and wearing a red knee-length suit, smiled benignly at the initiate, the drummers, the dancers, the follies of the gods.

"The drums revved up. Elegguá, god of the crossroads, had finished giving spiritual advice to a white-garbed novice and was now talking to another one in a more severe tone of voice. Suddenly, Oggun rushed toward a woman who was standing near the door and tried to push her way out of the room. Two officiaries went to divert him, like rodeo clowns corralling a Brahma bull. The warrior god looked around, still shaking and dancing. The drums kept beating. The chanting never stopped. Men, women, children, gods, everyone danced."

At some point in his life a santero will be initiated in an elaborate ceremony at the home of another initiate. At that time he becomes devoted to one particular orisha, just as many Catholics have a favorite saint. The initiate is considered to be reborn as a child of that orisha, and the orisha becomes a permanent part of the santero's personality.

In her excellent book on the subject, *Santeria: African Magic in Latin America* (Crown, 1973), Migene Gonzalez-Wippler explains:

"The cult of Santeria is a curious mixture of the magic rites of the Yorubas and the traditions of the Catholic church. All the legends and historical arguments that surround the lives of Jesus, Mary, and the Catholic saints are of great importance to the santero, as these data serve to delineate the personalities of the saints, making it easier to identify them with the appropriate Yoruba gods. But although the santero often finds his way to the Catholic church for an occasional mass, his sporadic visits are usually prompted by ulterior motives; namely, he may need some holy water for a spell, or a piece of the consecrated host, or maybe some candle wax with which to harm an enemy. For, in spite of the influence of the Catholic church,

Santeria is mostly primitive magic, and its roots are deeply buried in the heart of Africa, the ancestral home of the Yoruba people."

That this process of syncretism should occur is not really surprising. Teresita Pedraza, a professor of sociology and anthropology at Florida International University, and an expert on Santeria and Palo Mayombe, explains:

"The African religious mentality is that religions are not exclusive. They believe that every god has power. That's why when the African came to the new world it was easy for him to incorporate the gods of the white man. Today if you go to the home of a santero or a palero [practitioner of Palo Mayombe] you will find a figure of Buddha, or religious figure from the American Indian culture, or ornaments from other religions. They believe that all of these people have powers.

"And they respect other people's religions. Let's say you are Jewish and you go to a Santeria priest. Many people who are not santeros do. The priest might tell you that your problem is that your grandfather died three years back and you have not paid him enough respect and he's angry with you. The priest will pick up on the fact that you are Jewish, so what you have to do is go to the temple and pray for him. If you are Jewish, he is not going to send you to a Santeria *botánica* to buy candles. If you are Catholic, you will be told to arrange a special mass, and so forth."

Until recently Santeria got little notice in the U.S. and Canada. About the only time outsiders even heard the word was when some indignant

citizens discovered that the santeros had ritualistically been sacrificing chickens in the neighborhood
and made a big fuss about it. The resulting publicity tended to leave the public with an image of
santeros as a small group of people who spend most
of their time lopping off the heads of chickens and
sprinkling the blood around for good luck.

In fact, with a hundred million adherents worldwide (if you include the Africans, who, of course,
would not use the Catholic saints or the word
"Santeria"), this religion has about eight times the
number of adherents that Judaism claims. With its
recent emergence into the middle class of Latin
Americans, particularly in Florida, New York, and
New Jersey, Santeria has found its way into the
general popular culture in the form of movies and
fiction.

In 1987, for example, director John Schlesinger
made a film called *The Believers,* starring Martin
Sheen, and featuring Jimmy Smits. The film, which
is about a New York City cult that sacrifices children to gain money and power, clearly bases much
of its ritualism on Santeria. Afro-Caribbean religions also play a big part in the recent movies *Angel
Heart* and *The Serpent and the Rainbow.*

In *Black Moon* (Ballantine, 1989), a recently
published mystery by Alison Drake, the island of
Tango Key is the setting for a series of murders tied
to Palo Mayombe. Although Drake has fiction-
alized the legend of the black moon that is central
to her story, she says the descriptions of rites and
practices with Santeria and Palo Mayombe are
factual, drawn from her observations of such ritu-

als. And this book is just one of the many works of popular fiction that use the milieu of Santeria and Palo Mayombe the way writers of earlier decades used to turn to the Mafia for novel settings.

Perhaps one reason that these Afro-Caribbean religions are becoming popular with creators of fiction both on film and in books is that, because of the magic, they lend themselves quite easily to portrayals of villainy at a time when old stereotypical villains are fading. In publishing and in filmmaking, Russians, for example, are out as villains; they've lost their potency because of glasnost. Also, and perhaps more troubling, these religious contexts make credible particularly bizarre and harsh crimes at a time when simple murder is so common in real life that it is no longer compelling in fiction. Of course there are just so many films and books that can come out before people object to the way such sensationalistic treatments misrepresent a culture, just as Mafia films misrepresented Italian Americans. But in the meantime, in the wake of the Matamoros tragedy, we should expect more films and novels dealing with Santeria and Palo Mayombe.

When discussing a little-known religion, it is tempting to describe it in terms of one that is well-known. That might be easy with Santeria if Catholicism were the dominant influence, but in fact the Catholic influence is slight and on the wane. Santeria is best understood as an African religion and more easily explained if we talk about the ways in which it does not fit the Judeo-Christian model of what religion is.

In Santeria, for example, there is nothing equivalent to the Sabbath, because the religion cannot be sorted out from the rest of life the way Sunday is sorted out from the week.

"Santeria is a way of life," says Professor Pedraza. "Everything has meaning. Everything, negative or positive, has to be taken in the context of the religion. If you have a minor accident, or you receive word of an accident, it will be seen as someone working against you. If it is a positive thing, it will be seen as a sign of good luck from a guardian angel. Everything has meaning. The santero's life is far more religious than we can even imagine. Let's say you take an improper left turn, you get a ticket. That will be placed in the context of evil working against you. It will be taken that you have displeased the gods, and it will require that you do something about it. It is a sign that worse will happen to you if you do not immediately rearrange whatever caused it."

The idea of a church is also largely irrelevant to Santeria.

"Santeros worship at home," says Professor Mercedes Sandoval, of Miami-Dade Community College. "You have to worship where your sacred objects are. If a santero would go to church, he would have to take his sacred objects with him."

Perhaps the most stunning difference between Santeria and Christianity or Judaism is that Santeria is generally perceived to be amoral. Though certain behaviors are prohibited to certain people, there is no overall value system, no universal rules concerning sex, drinking, drugs, lying, etc.

"Santeria has no moral stance," says Professor Sandoval. "It doesn't make judgments in your life, it doesn't say no to anything. Santeria takes you where you are at."

Professor Pedraza says, "The concept of good or bad resides pretty much within the individual practitioners; it is not a function of the religion. Now, if you have a middle-class santero who works a normal job and raises kids just like everybody else, his values are reinforced by his peers, not the religion. You can do anything in Santeria and you can cleanse yourself. If a lady comes to see a santero, let's say, and her husband has another woman and she wants harm to come to that woman, the santero will work his magic to bring the woman harm and that woman becomes sick, let us say. All the santero has to do later on is some kind of cleansing ritual for himself and that passes the blame on to the person who came to him. He is only an agent for the harm."

To understand Pedraza's story we need to realize that she is using the word "santero" here in the sense of a santero priest, and the woman who comes to him would correctly be identified as a "client." A client may or may not be a practitioner of Santeria, but is a person who asks the santero priest to bring magic into the client's personal life.

"The Santeria priest has his clientele and his religious followers," Professor Pedraza explains. "The clientele is composed of anyone who goes to him for a reading and magic divination, usually in times of crisis. A client might show up often or only once in four years, because he wants a new job or a new lover or has a health problem. These people are not santeros. The clientele are the people who go to a santero priest in Miami. They are the same people who, if they lived in Maine, they would go to a medium or a tarot card reader."

This magic, which Migene Gonzalez-Wippler calls "sympathetic magic" and "jungle magic adapted to city living," has made Santeria and other African religions, such as Palo Mayombe and voodoo, very attractive to criminals, and there is a rising incidence of crimes that have an Afro-Caribbean religious component.

Robert Fiallo is a police officer with the Metro-Dade police department in Miami, and he is a student of sociology who has taken a special interest in this kind of crime. He suggests that criminals are attracted to the divination system found in Santeria because it differs from prayer in one important respect: the divination system does not differentiate between good and evil, whereas prayer in the Judeo-Christian tradition is not used to bring harm to others.

"You can't go into a synagogue and invoke God to have someone drop dead," Fiallo says. "You can't go to a Catholic priest and say, 'I'd like to have my boss keel over at his desk because he's giving me a hard time.' And you can't ask to have God protect your shipment of cocaine that's coming in. In Santeria and Palo Mayombe you can do these things."

While Santeria is generally considered to be amoral, even by the santeros, its amorality is an idea that becomes shaky under closer scrutiny. For one thing, the idea of displeasing the gods, as in Pedraza's incorrect-left-turn example, certainly implies moral judgment. One way to displease the gods would be to violate the eleven commandments of Obatala, father of the Yoruban gods. The commandments sound a lot like the biblical Ten Commandments and they are certainly not value free:

1. You will not steal.
2. You will not kill, except in self-defense and for your sustenance.
3. You will not eat human flesh.
4. You will live in peace among yourselves.
5. You will not covet your neighbor's properties.
6. You will not curse my name.
7. You will honor your father and your mother.
8. You will not ask more than I can give you, and you will be content with your faith.
9. You will neither fear death nor take your own life.
10. You will teach my commandments to your children.
11. You will respect and obey my laws.

Also, within the divination system there are various taboos associated with the individual gods who are assigned as spiritual guides to santeros.

"When you are initiated into Santeria, you are assigned heavenly parents in addition to your earthly parents," Professor Pedraza says. "You do not choose the gods, they choose you. When you go to the santero priest, he only asks your name and your date of birth."

Pedraza, however, has her suspicions about how these gods are assigned to individual santeros.

"Changó, for example, is a male warrior. He is a lover, a man who has five or six women, who likes to dance. However, his children cannot drink. If Changó is determined to be your father through the complex divination system, you cannot drink because if you drink, he is watching. Likewise, the daughter of certain deities can have numerous marriages and lots of men, no problem. The daughters of other deities cannot do that.

"My own interpretation is that if you have problems with drinking, your father is going to turn out to be Changó. I think it is a case of the priest being a wise person, and when you start dealing with human nature on a daily basis, consulting with fifteen or twenty people a day, I think after a couple of years if a woman walks in, you can figure out what her problem is."

Not surprisingly, this religion, with its animal sacrifices and its magic rituals, inspires derision and hostility. Some people, including former believers, say it is not a religion at all and that it should be done away with.

Robert Fiallo says, "I think people get bent out of shape over the chicken sacrifices because it is not sanitized. It's more like the old days when we lived in an agrarian society and you simply went into the barnyard and killed an animal. We don't have that now. You go into the meat section of a supermarket. Everything looks good, everything smells good, it's packaged in plastic, you don't see the blood. It's sanitized. We're uncomfortable with the idea of religious people simply cutting the head off a chicken or killing an animal without all this sanitizing.

"In the United States we have an ecclesiastical religious ceremony. A professional clergyman will conduct all the rites. You stand up, you sit down, you stand up, you sit down, sing this hymn, do this, do that. In Santeria, people actually become the clergy, if you want to call it that. They can sacrifice animals, they can perform divination rituals."

Officer Fiallo is not a santero and never has been. Born in Cuba, he has lived in the U.S. since he was four. But as a Miami police officer, he deals every day with the Cuban and non-Cuban community, and he is sensitive to the bigotry between the groups. To make a point about how suspicious and hostile nonsanteros can be, Fiallo tells this story:

"I get a call to go to the south end of the county, to a Latin neighborhood. An Anglo woman complains. She says go to a house about a half a block away and check on the welfare of a little girl. She says, 'I don't know what these people are into. I think it's that devil worship stuff, Santeria. I hear the girl scream bloody murder a couple of times a week, I can hear her in the afternoon, screaming.' So I pull up to the house, a very nice house with a nice lawn, and inside the large picture window is a big five-foot figurine of Saint Lazarus, or Babalu-Ayé, as he is known in Santeria, wearing a big maroon cape, very elaborate. And also there's a figure of a little black boy sitting down with a little fishing pole, and he's wearing overalls and he's got a little hat. These things are sold commercially and they are used to represent one of the lesser spirits in Santeria.

"So I know it's a santero who lives there. I knock on the door. A woman comes to the door and you can see that she's naked. She kind of hides behind the door to talk to me. She has some syrupy material in her hair and some kind of herbs or grasses clinging to her shoulders. I can smell violet water, which is a type of cologne frequently used in cleansing rituals. I say, 'I'm here to check on a report about a little girl screaming, to see if she's all right.' The woman says, 'The girl is fine, I'll bring her out and you can see for yourself.' She comes out a few minutes later with the little girl. The girl is maybe three years old and buck naked. She's got the same type of syrup in her hair and the herbs on her shoulders. She looks like she's been anointed, dipped into a liquid of some type. I'm looking her over for signs of abuse. She looks fine, healthy, well fed. She's smiling, and you can see that she's been crying. So it's obvious that this woman has been giving the girl some sort of ritual cleansing, which is typical in Santeria, herbs and honey to wash the evil away. And the kid was screaming just like any kid screams when he doesn't want a bath. This seems weird and cruel to outsiders, but it's no different than if you go to church to see a baby baptized and they cry."

Fiallo, who lectures to law enforcement agencies around the country about religious systems and crime, says that some illegal activities are associated with Santeria and Palo Mayombe, but suggests that most of the criticism of Santeria is hypocritical.

"We have a tendency to compare this religion to other religious systems," he says. "In our Judeo-Christian culture it's absurd for us to think in terms of blood sacrifice, which is quite common in Cuba. I can take you to certain cemeteries on any given day and we can find the remains of dozens of animals that have been used in sacrificial rites, goats, turtles . . . I have found a human skull in a cemetery. It's not uncommon to find these things in Miami, and you can pretty much link them back to the Afro-Caribbean religions. But the danger lies in condemning the whole religion. What are you doing when you receive communion? Communion is symbolic cannibalism. The Bible tells you you cannot consume blood because blood is the life force. In Judaism you have to kosher something because it is the life force. In the African-based religions, you use the blood *because* it is the life force. So what's the difference?"

The difference, in Hialeah, Florida, has been significant in recent months. Ernesto Pichardo, a Santeria priest, has opened a Santeria church, the Church of the Lukumi Babalu-Ayé, in an attempt to make Santeria more visible and more accessible, and the Hialeah city council is not happy about it. The council has banned animal sacrifices, citing Chapter 828 of the Florida Statutes, which prohibits "cruelty to animals." The santeros say it is their religious right to perform sacrifices.

When Pichardo began his church, he was hardly the religious primitive fresh out of the jungle that many nonsanteros would like to think. A good-looking young man, married to an anthropologist whom he met when she came to study with him, he lived in a Dade County condominium, drove a BMW, watched videos on his VCR, and liked to read books on psychology.

"We are normal, average people," says his wife, Lourdes. "Just because our religion happens to be a little different doesn't mean that everything has to be different. Our religion happens to be a little more bizarre than some of the neighbors'."

Pichardo has made it his mission to fight prejudice against Santeria, and after the bodies were discovered at Matamoros, he was kept busy trying to educate the press.

"Because Constanzo was a Cuban, some people very quickly stated that Santeria was being practiced," Pichardo told the *Miami Herald*. He was concerned that the damage had already been done. Stereotyping had set in. "People not knowledgeable of what Santeria is are expressing disgust with Santeria," he said. His concern was understandable. To condemn Santeria for the actions of Constanzo would be like damning all of Christiandom for the church burnings and lynchings committed by a few self-professed Christian Klansmen.

While Robert Fiallo agrees that santeros are for the most part good, law-abiding people, he implies that there is a tendency by leading santeros to dismiss any Santeria evil as not being Santeria at all.

"The people who talk about Santeria cover the spectrum," he says. "There are the people who say it's not a legitimate religion, that it's bad and so forth. But there are others who only see the good side of it, and the first thing they will tell you when Santeria is used in a crime is that it's not Santeria, that someone is using a bastardized version of Santeria for evil purposes. Well, what is Santeria? How can you tell? There's really no written word, like the Bible. It's all word of mouth and it's very susceptible to the individual practitioner putting in his two cents. The individual practitioner has tremendous control over the input and the result. For example, it is not unusual to have cleansing rituals for narcotics."

Charles Wetli is deputy chief medical examiner for Dade County and a professor of pathology at the University of Miami. Rafael Martinez is administrative officer of the Dade-Miami Criminal Justice Council. Both men are nationally recognized experts on Afro-Caribbean religions. (After the bodies were found in Matamoros, Texas law enforcement agencies considered the credentials of thirty experts around the country. Martinez was the man they chose to help them with their investigation.) They agree that Santeria can have a dark side and still be Santeria.

Writing in the *Journal of the Florida Medical Association* (August, 1983), they note:

"Because Santeria does not address a specific moral code as in the Judeo-Christian tradition, it is frequently found in association with criminal activities. Drug dealers, for example, not infrequently have elaborate statues and other depictions of Santeria in their homes, and Ochosi (god of hunting and owner of traps) is propitiated and honored among some criminal and socially deviant groups to avoid incarceration or obtain release from jail. Hence, Santeria, while predominantly a white or neutral magic religion, does have a component of malevolent sorcery and is invoked by criminal elements. This should not be construed, however, to suggest that Santeria promotes malevolent or criminal activities, but that it may simply be used by such persons to promote their already established intentions."

One effect of the Matamoros case was to lure many santeros out from under the veil of secrecy that has been characteristic of the religion ever since the Yoruban slaves started worshiping against the wishes of their masters. One night soon after the cult murders hit the press, a group of suburban Miami santeros, hoping to dispel public misconceptions about their religion, opened one ritual to reporters. Here is how reporter Liz Balmaseda described part of the evening's events in the *Miami Herald* (April 21, 1989):

"The 38-year-old initiate is ill again and her *madrina* . . . says a sacrifice is required to cleanse her of misfortune. As she enters the sacrifice room . . . the santero priest and his assistant bring in the first goat. His mouth and ears tied with string, the animal quietly whines.

"The initiate takes a mouthful of shredded coconut and spits it upon the goat's face and kisses his ears. She rubs the animal's face across her breasts.

Around her, the believers chant in Yoruba, *'Kosi iku, kosi arun kosi araye.'* ('Let us not see troubles, early death, or unnecessary illness.')

"The animal barely squirms when Willie Ramos pierces its neck. The knife slips out red, and blood drips in a stream upon the offering. The animal, headless, twitches spastically. Finally, it is still.

"Later, the chicken's neck is cut and bled in the same fashion. The santero pours a box of salt on the goat's head, then douses the offering with honey. The initiate plucks the bird's feathers and scatters them.

"Then the chanting stops; the offering pots are placed in a corner. The goat and chicken are cleaned, skinned, chopped, and placed in marinade.

"A costumed santera mops the blood from the linoleum floor. It comes right off."

Later in her article Balmaseda quotes Willie Ramos, the priest who performed the ceremony:

"These sacrifices are our communion with the saints. Then we clean the animals and eat them. So why the constant persecution of Santeria? How many animals are killed every day to feed the people of the United States?"

It was in this controversial religion that Adolfo Constanzo was brought up by Aurora, a woman who fervently believed in it. If tradition was followed, the boy was taught that the magic of the santero was neither good nor evil; it was simply a means to an end. Typically, he would see that the santero priest could use elaborate rituals to attempt such feats as curing illness, getting a job, attracting a lover, or even bringing on the death of an enemy. Under normal circumstances he would learn that the spell-casting of the santero should only be used as white magic, not to hurt people. However, it seems safe to say that Adolfo Constanzo did not grow up in "normal circumstances."

As a boy Adolfo was probably initiated into Santeria by his mother, who filled the role of sponsor, or *madrina.* Aurora reportedly has presented herself as a Santerian priestess, though it is not known whether or not she has gone through the years of training required to become a true priest or priestess, and it certainly appears that her social skills and sensitivity are not what one would hope for in a personal counselor.

Young Constanzo, we can assume, was given the *collare,* a necklace that would protect him from evil. At his initiation ceremony Constanzo's head would be cleansed by his *madrina* with a paste that is made of ground coconut meat, cocoa butter, and powdered eggshell. Also as part of the ceremony, animals would be sacrificed, a ritual that by this time would be quite familiar to Constanzo. The choice of animals to be killed varies. It would depend on which orisha was being invoked to take possession of Adolfo.

There is some evidence that Constanzo was dedicated to the orisha Oggun. Philip Carlo, a New York writer and an expert on the occult, says, "Constanzo had all of Oggun's implements, i.e., a horseshoe, a chain, railroad spikes, things of metal."

In her book, Gonzalez-Wippler says of Oggun:

"God of war and iron. His origin is obscure. Some legends say that he was conceived of the union of Obatala and Oddudua, but this is debated by many babalawos. He eats dogs and is the patron of ironworkers. Before going to war, the Yorubas used to sacrifice to him a human victim or a black dog."

Constanzo, apparently, took it all to heart, and he spent much of his childhood on errands for his mother, running to and from the *botánicas,* the religious goods stores that can be found in all Cuban neighborhoods.

(The *botánicas* sell spiritual incense, antispirit potions, candles, herbs, ancestral dolls, and other Santerian paraphernalia. Joseph Murphy, writing in *The Encyclopedia of Religion* (MacMillan, 1987), notes: "The presence of Santeria in a given neighborhood may be gauged by the profusion of *botánicas* . . . In 1981, there were at least eighty *botánicas* in Miami, Florida, and more than a hundred in New York City.")

However, Aurora apparently felt that Santeria alone was not enough to meet all of her needs for her son. When Adolfo was fourteen, his mother sent him to study Palo Mayombe under the tutelage of a mayombero, or black witch.

Palo Mayombe, which means "way of the black witch," is the black magic of the Congo. It can be traced back not to the Yoruba people of Nigeria, but to slaves from the Congo, who also tried to preserve their religion by taking on aspects of the Spanish Catholic culture. However, the paleros, as believers are called, were also influenced by the Yorubas, so that the Palo Mayombe syncretism (that is, the reconciliation of differing religious beliefs) included not just aspects of Catholicism, but also aspects of Santeria.

Palo Mayombe has its own pantheon, but because of syncretism many of its gods correspond to Santeria orishas, which in turn correspond to Catholic saints. For example, Oggun, the orisha that Philip Carlo believes Constanzo was devoted to, is understood as Zarabanda in Palo Mayombe or Saint Peter in Roman Catholicism. The supreme deity in Palo Mayombe is known as Guindoki, also as Chamalongo and Nsambi, and he would be the equivalent of Olofi in Santeria.

As with Santeria, much of the Palo Mayombe ritual is conducted for magical reasons. Through various and complicated procedures, the palero believes he can protect himself, solve problems, acquire lovers or money, make his enemies go mad, or kill people.

Some people say that Palo Mayombe is "the dark side of Santeria." Others say that that is misleading and that Palo Mayombe must be viewed as a completely different Afro-Caribbean religion. Wetli and Martinez, in their medical journal article, see it this way:

"Because of the acculturative and syncretic processes which took place over several centuries, the rituals and myths of Palo Mayombe are frequently associated with the practitioners of Santeria. Indeed, many santeros claim they have also been "Rayado en Palo" [initiated into the Palo Mayombe cult]. Religious paraphernalia typical of Santeria and those characteristic of Palo Mayombe

115

may be found in the same home, but in different locations of the residence. Despite the historical and symbolic associations with Santeria, Palo Mayombe has certain distinguishing features. Most importantly, the myths and rituals of Palo Mayombe are centered about the spirit of the dead (kiyumba). In most instances, the magic is used to inflict misfortune (insanity, divorce, etc.) or death upon an enemy or the enemy of a client."

The most discussed distinction between Santeria and Palo Mayombe, and certainly the most relevant one in connection with Constanzo, is the latter's alleged wickedness.

Wetli and Martinez write: "In contrast to Santeria, which is predominantly used for good or neutral purposes, Palo Mayombe is primarily oriented towards malevolent sorcery. While many depictions and symbols in Palo Mayombe appear identical to Santeria, devotion to *brujería*, the use of human remains, and other features distinguish this cult from other African-Caribbean religions."

Officer Fiallo has investigated a number of murders involving both Santeria and Palo Mayombe. He says, "Is Palo more evil? I think Palo deals with a realm of a more evil nature. One of its central themes is that the practitioner owns the spirit of a dead individual. That's why they need to have human remains. So you're dealing in the realm of the dead and that's a more negative aspect to begin with."

Migene Gonzalez-Wippler, in her book, also seems to be saying that Palo Mayombe exists mostly in the shadows of evil. A mayombero (black witch), which is what Constanzo would eventually claim to be, is, according to Gonzalez-Wippler, "feared like a devil incarnate. His power is believed to be real and awesome. A mayombero is not a common delinquent. He can maim and kill with impunity because he cannot be punished by established laws. The mayombero does not invoke the orishas for his evil works, for an orisha is a force of light that can be used only for just purposes. He uses only negative and evil entities for his fearful bilongos or black magic spells."

(One should note that Migene Gonzalez-Wippler is herself a santero and understandably protective of her religion. Not all scholars would agree with her statement that orishas can be "used only for just purposes.")

Professor Pedraza, on the other hand, says that paleros are getting a bad rap.

"It's not correct to say that Palo Mayombe is the dark side of Santeria," she says. "Santeria has a dark side if the santero chooses, and it is perceived to be just as powerful as Palo. All African religions can be used for good or evil. Most of the paleros are good, law-abiding people. This Constanzo thing takes place thousands of miles away from Miami. There are over five thousand paleros in Miami, and they have never seen anything like this. Certainly some paleros are linked with drugs, numbers, and prostitution. It has always had that kind of social stigma. But if you are into drugs or illegal activity, if you are living on the margin, you are going to seek protection more than anybody else, and you can't go to the Catholic church to pray for protection tonight for a shipload of cocaine. You can't go to the priest and tell him that I am in love with my best friend's wife and I want to see how I can get her over to my place. But that doesn't mean that all paleros are evil. How come with five thousand paleros in Miami, this man Constanzo couldn't even get a following in Miami?"

While it would be difficult to imagine a Catholic turning to Judaism and continuing to go to mass and take communion, there is no such contradiction in Aurora Constanzo's practicing Santeria and Palo Mayombe at the same time. Many people do. Followers of African religions tend to respect the gods of other African religions, and also to fear their magic.

Adolfo's initiation into Palo Mayombe would have been no less bizarre than his initiation into Santeria.

If the dogma was carefully followed, young Adolfo would have slept for seven nights under a sacred tree. Then he would have walked to a cemetery, carrying a new set of clothes, dug up an existing grave, and buried the clothes in it. During the twenty-one days that the clothes remained interred, Constanzo would take a number of purifying herb baths. When he returned to the cemetery, he would dig up his clothes and put them on. Then he would be led to a sacred tree where the gathered witnesses would invoke the spirits of the dead. He would be given a crown of leaves, which, it is said, would attract the spirits of the dead who would take possession of him. He would also receive a candle on a white dish, and a human tibia, taken from a corpse. The tibia is the bone that connects a person's knee to his ankle, and the mayombero uses it as a scepter.

After this ceremony the initiate, according to Gonzalez-Wippler, "is then declared a full-fledged mayombero and is able to conduct all the fearful ceremonies of the cult."

But Miss Gonzalez-Wippler notes that before someone like Constanzo can truly call himself a mayombero, he must protect himself by preparing the legendary cauldron of the Congos, which is known as a nganga.

"This frightful concoction," she writes, "is so violently feared in Santeria that no one dares speak of it except in whispers. The method of preparation of a nganga has been a closely guarded secret for centuries."

However, Gonzales-Wippler reveals in her book that a mayombero did tell her the ingredients and the uses of the cauldron, and her explanation is frighteningly prophetic in the light of what we now know about the discovery at Matamoros.

"The mayombero waits until the moon is propitious, and then he goes to a cemetery with an assistant. Once there, he sprinkles rum in the form of a cross over a prechosen grave. The grave is opened, and the head, the toes, the fingers, the ribs, and the tibias of the corpse are removed. These graves are chosen ahead of time, and the mayombero usually knows the identity of the cadaver, which is known as kiyumba. They are usually recent graves, as the mayombero insists on having a head in which the brain is still present, however decayed. He believes that the brain of the kiyumba can think and thus 'act' better. The choice kiyumbas are those belonging to very violent persons, especially those of criminals and of the insane, for the purposes of the mayombero are generally to commit acts of death and destruction. The bodies of white persons are also greatly favored, as the mayombero believes that the brain of the white person is easier to influence than that of a black man and that it will follow instructions better."

(While the use of body parts might imply grave-robbing or other illegal activities, it's important to note that a palero could make a nganga without breaking the law. There is, for example, an occult supply house in Pennsylvania that will sell you a human skull, a left arm, a right arm, a left leg, etc., all legal medical specimens.)

The proper preparation of the cauldron is elaborate and precise, and it includes, along with the human brain and other body parts, insects, spices, and the body of a small black dog to help the spirit find its victims.

After the "killing shack" was discovered at Rancho Santa Elena, pictures of Constanzo's cauldron, his nganga, appeared in newspapers all over the world. It would become, perhaps, the most lasting symbol of El Padrino's terrible crimes. While it is probably true, as Teresita Pedraza says, that "Constanzo was a sociopath and he would have murdered people even if he was a Methodist," it is equally true that he was a practitioner of these Afro-Caribbean religions, and that the power of his own personality combined with the seductive magical religion that he preached was persuasive enough to turn several young people into murderers.

SIX

The Murders

Adolfo de Jesús Constanzo was born on November 1, 1962, in Miami. His mother was a teenaged Cuban immigrant in Florida. His father was gone within a year. When Adolfo was still a baby, his mother took him to Puerto Rico where she married her second husband. There Adolfo took up tennis and served as an altar boy in a Roman Catholic church. When he was ten, the family returned to Miami, and shortly after that Adolfo's stepfather died of cancer. Aurora married again, but her third husband did not get along well with Constanzo, and the conflict between stepfather and stepson played a large part in Aurora's divorce from her third husband.

Adolfo, the oldest of four children, was a loner even as a kid. He had few friends and found out early in life that kids did not want to play with him because they were frightened of his mother and the strange religion she allegedly practiced.

At age fourteen, according to his mother, Adolfo

showed strong evidence of psychic powers. He could predict the future.

Adolfo went through ninth grade, then he quit school and started working odd jobs. But there was about him an aura, a sense that he was meant for bigger things. He was a good-looking young man, red haired, charismatic. By the time he reached his twenties he had gotten occasional work as a model.

Constanzo was also a neatness nut.

"As a child he always loved to be clean, with his clothes ironed and very neat," his mother told Melinda Henneberger of the *Dallas Morning News* after her son was dead. "Practically from the time he was one year old he always kept his robe by his bed to put it on if he got up in the night."

There has been no evidence that Constanzo was involved with serious crime during his teenage years. He was, however, arrested twice for shoplifting in 1981, and one of those times it was for stealing a chainsaw.

In 1984, when Constanzo was twenty-two, he left Miami and moved, in his mother's words, "to explore new horizons in Mexico."

In Mexico City, police now believe, Constanzo managed to charm his way into the inner sanctums of the most ruthless drug-running gangsters in the country and the powerful politicians who protected them. Soon he was selling drugs and hanging around with people who were much more powerful than the Matamoros-based Hernandez gang, whose ton-a-week marijuana operation, which Constanzo would eventually take over, was regarded as relatively small potatoes. Though Constanzo was a homosexual who became a familiar figure in the gay bars of the Zona Rosa (the pink zone, a trendy neighborhood of boutiques, sidewalk cafés, discotheques, and nice restaurants in Mexico City), he again fathered a child, according to his mother. The boy, now four, is also named Adolfo and lives with Aurora in Miami. Around the Zona Rosa, Constanzo earned a reputation as a man of mystery and danger. He attracted followers. He became a cult leader. Constanzo, it was said, was not a man you would want to offend.

He also earned a reputation as a psychic. Constanzo, it was said, could advise you well about finances, romance, whatever you wanted to know. He soon became a kind of psychic to the stars, charging enormous fees to tell some of Mexico's biggest celebrities whether or not to get married, buy land, take the role, make the record.

Oscar Athie, a well-known Mexican singer, denies that he was ever involved with Constanzo's cult, but he says that El Padrino tried to extort money from him because he refused to give El Padrino a concert in Miami, and would not pay for one of Constanzo's ritual cleansings.

Athie says he went to Miami to discuss a concert proposal with Constanzo and turned it down.

"When I returned to Mexico," he says, "they kept calling me, harassing and threatening me at my home in Acapulco. They were telling me that if I didn't perform for them I would have bad luck in my career. I had to change my phone number. I despise everything they have done, all of their qualities. I am a Catholic, and I don't believe in their religion."

Constanzo made a fortune from his celebrity clients and his drug deals. He took to wearing expensive jewelry, driving a Mercedes, and buying presents for his boyfriends.

People were drawn to Adolfo, but not because he was a lot of laughs. He was an intense, serious individual, "a very serious, serious, serious guy," one of his followers told the *Dallas Morning Herald*. The people who were pulled into his force describe him variously as "enigmatic," "mesmerizing," and "exciting." Many who knew him are convinced that he had the power of precognition. Others who knew him are just as convinced that he will be reincarnated.

Constanzo, ever the devoted son, sent money home to his mother regularly and often flew to Miami to be with her.

"The mother used to brag about how powerful her kid was; he was like another Messiah," says Ernesto Pichardo, the Santerian priest in Hialeah. But Pichardo notes that by the time that Constanzo was controlling the Hernandez drug-smuggling operation, even Aurora was alarmed. "She was concerned that people were being killed by her son's ring," he says.

In Mexico City, Constanzo was, apparently, as zealous as ever about his religion of magic. His magnetic personality drew many people, mostly young, to his way of thinking. While he was charging the rich and famous thousands for spiritual cleansings, he performed a number of spiritual cleansings that, it seems, were only for the purpose of adding to his flock. One of his converts, former fashion model Maria del Rocio Cuevas, who at forty-three was the oldest member of his cult, helped recruit others, a job that in Matamoros and Brownsville would be given to Sara Aldrete.

There's no way of saying when Adolfo committed his first murder or what psychic demons led him to do it. We know that much of the Palo Mayombe ritual requires human body parts, which traditionally are bought from medical schools or stolen from graveyards and funeral homes. And we also know, because of the Matamoros discovery, that by 1988 Constanzo was sacrificing humans to get body parts. But we don't know when Constanzo crossed that border between religion and murder. Certainly it is possible that Adolfo had performed ritualistic murders long before he got to Mexico. In any case, Mexico City has at least two murder cases before April of 1988 that seem to bear the fingerprints of Adolfo de Jesús Constanzo. In 1986, Mexican police discovered six mutilated bodies floating in the Zumpango River. Mexico's Deputy Attorney General Abraham Polo says that Constanzo was one target of a police investigation of those murders.

Constanzo has also been named as the murderer of an alleged transvestite named Edgar, whom Constanzo called Claudia Yvette. Omar Francisco Orea Ochoa, a student at a prestigious Mexico City college, came under the Constanzo spell at age sixteen. He is a former lover and follower of El

Padrino. He says that Constanzo picked up Claudia in the Zona Rosa and went with him to an apartment, where Constanzo killed the man. Constanzo and Orea then carved Claudia up and shoved the pieces into a plastic bag. Orea has not said that the Claudia killing was related to Constanzo's drug-smuggling efforts.

Constanzo's dope dealings brought him to Matamoros from time to time, and on one of those trips, in the summer of 1987, he met Sara Aldrete.

According to Sara, they met on a street in Matamoros. She was driving her father's car along the Avenido Alvaro Obregon when she met Adolfo, apparently at a stoplight. Constanzo, who was with his friend and lover, Martin Quintana, told Sara that he was from Miami and invited her to have a drink with them at Los Sombreros.

Sara was drawn to the handsome, and apparently wealthy, Constanzo. She had just been divorced from her husband and felt very low. He seemed to know a lot about the occult and that attracted her. In time they became lovers. Constanzo indoctrinated her, she says, into Santeria Cristiana, Christian Santeria. She says that when they first met, he never mentioned Palo Mayombe.

Constanzo read Sara's future in tarot cards and she was impressed by his accuracy. More and more she saw him as a leader and herself as a follower. Their romance ended when Constanzo confessed that he had not one other lover, but two of them. And that they were male. Here's how Sara retold the conversation on "The Reporters" television show after her arrest:

"It was around the twentieth that he told me that I was very nice to him and he didn't want to hurt me and that he wanted to tell the truth and he said, I have two lovers in Mexico. What kind of lovers? I asked him. Like, are you married? No, no, I'm not, he said. Oh, okay, I go. So, what's the problem? He goes, well, they're men."

Despite this detour in the relationship Sara and Constanzo remained close as friends, and she was as devoted to him as the rest of his followers. Soon Sara was helping to recruit new members of the cult. Her main recruiting tool was the film *The Believers*, directed by John Schlesinger and starring Martin Sheen. In the movie, a cult of New York society people have been sacrificing one child each to bring them good luck and riches. It's not clear exactly how the kids are being sacrificed, but a circle of ashes is always found around the sacrificial altar. Sheen plays Dr. Cal Jamison, a New York Police Department psychologist. His son Chris, played by Harley Cross, finds a shell in Central Park. The shell, apparently, has been used in some sort of ritual. We know, because chickens have been sacrificed nearby. By picking up the shell, little Chris has become some sort of "chosen one."

Sheen's character has a Spanish-speaking maid, and she knows that evil forces are at work, so she goes to work with her white magic of Santeria. She rubs chicken eggs over Chris. She dips crosses in glasses of water. She does her best, but Jamison thinks she's nuts, and he fires her.

Jamison finds out that his own father-in-law is

The shed at Rancho Santa Elena where the cult suspects claim their rituals took place.
(BRAD DOHERTY)

Items found in the cult's shed. The big pot is the *nganga*, alleged to be self-styled *mayombero* Adolfo Constanzo's source of power. The pot contains parts of a human brain, a dead turtle, blood, burnt cigars and various spices.
(JOE HERMOSA)

James Kilroy and his wife, Helen, at their son Mark's funeral. Mark's photograph appears in the lower right-hand corner.

(AP/WIDE WORLD PHOTOS)

From left to right, Bill Huddleston, Oran Neck, Bradley Moore, William Canant and Brent Martin outside the London Pub/Hard Rock Cafe in Matamoros, Mexico. Kilroy's friends—Huddleston, Moore and Martin—are here retracing their steps the night Mark disappeared for U.S. Customs Service investigator Oran Neck and U.S. Customs Service special agent William Canant.

(BRAD DOHERTY)

Three of the five cult members arrested on April 9, 1989. Left to right, they are Elio Hernandez Rivera, David Serna Valdez and Sergio Martinez. On the far right is Domingo Reyes, the caretaker who identified Mark's picture.

(DAVID ANTHONY PADILLA)

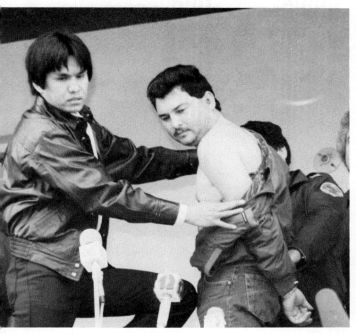

At a press conference on April 12, federal judicial police commandant Juan Benitez pulls aside the shirt of cult suspect Elio Hernandez Rivera to expose his shoulder, which bears markings made by Adolfo Constanzo. These markings allegedly designate Elio as an executioner in the drug smuggler's cult.

(AP/WIDE WORLD PHOTOS)

Cult suspect Sergio Martinez digs to uncover the grave of a thirteenth victim at Rancho Santa Elena.

Mexican police workers excavating victim's remains at
Rancho Santa Elena on April 11, 1989.

(JOE HERMOSA)

Mexican police worker removing victim's remains from grave site.
(JOE HERMOSA)

Mexican police workers examining remains of a body that has been exhumed.
(JOE HERMOSA)

Mexican police workers carrying victim's body to collection site at Rancho Santa Elena.

(JOE HERMOSA)

The body bags lined up in front of the suspected cult members' ritual shed. Later, the bodies were removed to various funeral homes for identification.

Cult suspect David Serna Valdez in the custody of Mexican police at Rancho Santa Elena.

(JOE HERMOSA)

Mexican police burn the cult suspects' shed at Rancho Santa Elena on April 23, 1989. Cameron County Sheriff Alex Perez, who accompanied Lt. George Gavito at the scene, told reporters they burned "the temple to show Adolfo de Jesus Constanzo that the police officers mean business." Constanzo was at that time still at large.

(FRANK ORDOÑEZ)

The apartment complex at Rio Sena 19 in Mexico City where Constanzo, Sara Aldrete and other suspected cult members were found on April 6, 1989.

(JIM BUDD)

Police agents in Mexico City arrest Alvaro de Leon Valdez, El Duby, after shootout with suspected members of cult at Rio Sena 19. El Duby later confessed that he had executed Constanzo and his bodyguard in compliance with the cult leader's own orders.

Arrested cult suspects at press conference in Mexico City on May 7, 1989. From left to right, they are Maria del Rocio Cuevas Guerra; Alvaro de Leon Valdez, El Duby; Omar Francisco Orea Ochoa; Maria de Lourdes Bueno Lopez; and Sara Aldrete.

Sara Aldrete as she appeared the day of our exclusive interview with her. She had at this time been in a prison in Mexico City for over ten weeks.

(JIM BUDD)

Adolfo de Jesus Constanzo, left, and his bodyguard and reported lover, Martin Quintana Rodriguez, in a photograph found in a police raid of Constanzo's Mexico City apartment.

part of the cult and is told that he can join, too, and achieve great power if he sacrifices his son.

(This goes to the heart of the Matamoros cult's belief. They believed that if they made human sacrifices, the gods would protect their drug-smuggling operation and protect them from the police. "They said they thought bullets would not hit them if they made the sacrifices," George Gavito says.)

Just as Jamison is, apparently, about to shove the ritual knife into his son, he turns and shoves it into a cultist. There follows a not-surprising Hollywood happy ending.

The movie is neither sophisticated nor particularly accurate in its portrayal of Santeria. Nonetheless, it helped persuade some young people, and Constanzo's cult grew. By one estimate there were twenty-four people in the cult by the time it was broken up, including some who were not benefiting from the proceeds of the drug smuggling. (Also, not all of those who helped smuggle drugs were into the religion.)

As mentioned, there are many stories about when and where Constanzo first formed his fatal alliance with Elio Hernandez. But it was perhaps at Constanzo's luxurious house in a middle-class neighborhood of Atizapan, eleven miles from the center of Mexico City, that he revealed himself as a mayombero. Atizapan was Constanzo's safe house. Here, right across the street from an elementary school, he and his four young male housemates lived behind a ten-foot, neatly whitewashed wall that surrounded the property. They had planted a garden there. They had installed five closed-circuit television cameras and a radar-controlled spotlight system that flooded the street with light at night whenever a car drove by. On the roof there was a large parabolic satellite antenna. In the yard there was a target riddled with bullet holes.

Yes, it would be here that Constanzo would have drawn Hernandez into his world of magic.

It is not hard to imagine Constanzo, the swaggering red-haired Cuban, strutting across the black-and-white-tiled floor of the living room, eyeing his guest, who would sit contentedly in the white leather furniture.

"Protection," Constanzo would say. "That is what you asked for, that is what you've got."

"Yes," Hernandez would say, and he would be pleased, for the money was flowing in, even if he did have to give half of it to this Cuban American.

"Did you ever wonder why?" Constanzo might say. He might eye Hernandez, thinking, this fellow is as young as all the others who follow me.

"Why?" Elio would say. "What do you mean why?"

"Why no harm comes to you. Why the police do not trouble you," Constanzo would say, savoring the secret that was only feet away from young Elio, behind the mirrored walls.

"I don't know," Elio would say.

"Brujería," Constanzo would whisper across the room. *"Brujería."*

"Brujería?" Elio would ask, perhaps excited,

perhaps frightened, perhaps both. He would lean forward, stare expectantly at his host. What was it about this young Cuban that was so mesmerizing? he would wonder.

"The gods help us," Constanzo would say. And then, "But of course, they must be paid."

In time he would move close to young Elio. He would stare at him with those eyes that had captured so many. He would raise a beckoning hand. "Come," he would say. And to the mirrored walls they would walk. Constanzo would pull back the mirrors. "See," he would say, and they would enter the hidden space, the altar that was there, secluded in the secret walls of Adolfo Constanzo's safe home.

(It would be in April of 1989 that Mexican police would come upon this secret altar, and there they would find candles and robes and a sword and something they called a devil doll.

"A devil doll," explains Anthony Zavaleta, "can come in many forms, but basically it is like a voodoo doll, a representation of a person you want to hurt or kill.")

Of course, only Elio knows for sure when and where Constanzo began to sway him toward Palo Mayombe. But we do know that a deal of some sort was made. That Constanzo offered drugs and protection, that he began to fly often to Brownsville, where he stayed at the Holiday Inn, that he went to Rancho Santa Elena to tend to the drug-smuggling business, that he was charismatic enough to take over the gang and, furthermore, to weave a spell over a number of young men and at least one young woman, and that for this young Cuban from America they were willing to torture, murder, and dismember fellow human beings.

The gang of drug smugglers and devotees that swarmed around Constanzo seemed to have no fear of being caught. Because they believed they had magic on their side, and also because they were, allegedly, bribing police, many of them spoke freely about being involved in illegal activities.

Serafin, for example, has been described by townspeople in Matamoros as a renegade who often boasted that he had local cops "on the take."

George Gavito says that the gang members went pretty much anyplace they pleased. "They ran with this group in Matamoros and did whatever they wanted," he says. "They were protected."

After the story hit the newspapers, one young man, whom we will call Peter because he wants to remain anonymous, recalled two incidents in which he ran into members of Constanzo's gang, though he didn't know at the time whom he was dealing with.

What follows is a description of those encounters based on Peter's recollection.

At three o'clock in the afternoon on a weekday in January 1989, Peter was sitting alone at a table in a lounge on Central Avenue in Brownsville. He was drinking a beer. A large group of men, about ten of them, came in. They were a rowdy-looking bunch. They smoked cigars, drank straight whisky. Some spoke Spanish, others spoke English, some mixed the languages. Most of the men walked to the back of the bar, where there were pool tables. Others came over and took tables near Peter.

"An old guy, about fifty, stands close to me," Peter says, "and a younger, good-looking guy stood next to him. And these guys were bragging about being in the Mafia, bragging to anyone who would listen. Besides me there were maybe two other people and a barmaid."

"So you're in the Mafia?" Peter said to the men. "Tell me, how do you do that without getting caught?"

"We have protection," said the older man, who seemed to be a Hispanic American. He was dark skinned, dark haired, dark eyed. "A shield," he added, lifting his arms high to indicate a shield.

"Oh, so you're the Godfather," Peter said.

"No," the man said. "I'm the godson."

"The godson? I've never heard of that."

"The Godfather's back there," the man said, gesturing to the area where the others were shooting pool. The man he pointed to, Peter realizes now, was Adolfo Constanzo.

Peter questioned the men about the shield. "They said we have a belief like voodoo," Peter says now. "They never mentioned Santeria or Palo Mayombe."

"Well," Peter said to them, "I practice a little magic myself."

The older man then walked over to Constanzo and came back with a notebook of unlined paper that had a collection of lines, circles, and stars drawn in it. (After Constanzo's death, Mexican police recovered his diary or book of spells.

133

Though its contents have not been revealed to the press, a source who has seen the book thinks it is probably the same book that Peter saw in the bar.)

"If you're into magic, you should be able to read this," the man said to Peter, showing him the book, but not allowing him to touch it.

Then the Godfather shouted from the back of the room in English, "If he can't read that, he's a fake." To Peter's shock, the Godfather was enraged. He stormed to the front part of the lounge, grabbed the book out of the older man's hands, and walked away.

"Constanzo jingled when he walked," Peter says now. "Charms or something. He sounded like he was wearing spurs."

Next the older man asked Peter what color candles he burned.

"White," Peter said.

"We burn black candles," the man said.

"Where do you practice?" Peter asked.

"Oh," the man said, "we have a little building outside Matamoros on a ranch." He also made some reference to a house in Mexico City.

The conversation soon ended and, later, when Constanzo started motioning his followers toward the door, he walked up to Peter and said to his gang, "He knows too much."

"Hey, don't worry about me," Peter said. "I won't say nothing. Just like Schultz on 'Hogan's Heroes.'"

Constanzo, surrounded by his men, looked at Peter strangely. Apparently he had no idea that "Hogan's Heroes" was a television show.

The older man said to Peter, "You better not tell anybody about us." Constanzo and the older man whispered something to each other, apparently in an argument, then they left.

Five minutes later, a long-haired young Mexican girl (apparently not Sara, by Peter's description) came in and said to Peter, "You've been talking to those guys? You know, they're dangerous, they're killers."

About a week later Peter was having a drink at the same lounge when four of the men came in. Constanzo was not with them, but the older man was. He recognized Peter, and again the bragging started.

The older man told Peter that in his belief goats and chickens were sacrificed.

"The older guy was mad that day about something," Peter says now. "He kept doing something with his head and his eyes glared and he asked me, 'What do I look like?' and I told him, 'You look like an old banty rooster.' He kept asking me, 'What do I look like?' and I kept saying a rooster or a chicken and that made him angry. Later I wondered if a chicken was the image for the devil or something."

Later in the conversation Peter asked the older man how the group got its power. The man walked over to a younger man, who reached into his pocket and pulled out a human ear.

Peter thought it was fake, made of rubber. But the older man said to the younger man, "Put that away. You're going to have to get rid of that thing because it's going to start to stink pretty soon."

When Peter told the group that he was part

Indian, they asked him if he knew how to scalp people.

"I don't know," Peter said.

"Well, we do," one of the men said. "Feel this." He held out a length of hair that was wrapped around his belt.

"Rabbit?" Peter asked.

"It's human hair," he was told.

According to statements made by the cultists, the first rituals involved only the sacrifice of animals, and only Constanzo, Serafin, and Sara participated.

Though the believers of Matamoros were dedicated to Constanzo, there is serious doubt about how well they understood the religion they were practicing. Sara says she was practicing Christian Santeria. Serafin seems even more confused.

After he was arrested, Serafin told George Gavito that his favorite movie was *The Believers.*

"I remember I didn't understand what he was telling me," Gavito says. "I said, 'Is it Santeria?' And he said, 'Yeah, yeah, Santeria, voodoo, man.' And then he kept on saying, *'The Believers, The Believers, The Believers.'*"

It was Elio Hernandez who explained to the police that it wasn't just Santeria that the cult practiced, but Palo Mayombe, too.

"Elio made [Serafin] Garcia a priest," Gavito says, "but Garcia didn't really know what it was he was practicing because all he had on his mind was that movie."

Apparently, Elio also didn't know the fine points

of his religion. When police asked him the name of his god, he said, "I don't know. The Godfather knows. He said he'd reveal that later." Elio also told police he was a Catholic.

Some of the cultists, it seems, were in the habit of calling their religion "voodoo." While voodoo does refer to a primitive African religion based on sorcery and brought to the Caribbean, it is more commonly used to describe African religion as it evolved among Haitians under the French, not Cubans under the Spanish.

As far as we know, all of the rituals done in the Matamoros area were done at the ranch. This was not simply because the shack was isolated and marijuana was stored on the farm.

"Traditionally Palo Mayombe is kept in a rustic-type shack outside the house," Robert Fiallo says. "The theory is that since Palo deals with the spirits of the dead, you do it outside. Santeria, the white magic, you do inside."

We don't know exactly when, but probably sometime during the autumn of 1988, Constanzo made his first Matamoros nganga. As noted, the nganga is, in Migene Gonzalez-Wippler's words, the "frightful concoction" that is "so violently feared that no one dares speak of it except in whispers." The nganga is the cauldron and all its dreadful contents. It gives the mayombero his power, and it is the center of Palo Mayombe ritual.

If Constanzo prepared his nganga properly (and from what was found at the shack, it appears that he did), he included a human skull, long bones from the legs of a human corpse, sticks from a

137

forest, sacred stones, feathers, railroad spikes, the bones and skulls of other animals, and small iron tools.

"The most important of these items are the sacred stones and the skull," write Wetli and Martinez in their journal article. "The stones are ritually 'fed' when the nganga is offered blood in a ceremony called simbankisi. The skull is especially referred to as the kiyumba, meaning spiritual substance or intelligence of the dead. The 'father' or 'mother' of the nganga interacts with his/her kiyumba by 'feeding,' 'punishing,' or making the nganga 'give birth' to initiates or new paleros. The skulls may be obtained from various sources. However, some mayomberos insist on a skull in which the brain is still present so the kiyumba can think and act better."

Among the additional ingredients of a properly prepared nganga, many of which were found in the shack at Santa Elena, are wax from a burnt candle, coins, ashes, a cigar butt, red pepper, blood, chili, garlic, ginger, onion, cinnamon, ants, worms, lizards, termites, bats, flies, a tarantula, a centipede, a wasp, and a scorpion.

As nasty as all this sounds, it is important to note that neither Gonzalez-Wippler nor Wetli and Martinez suggest that any widespread human sacrificing is occurring, and they make no references to torture. These aspects of the activities at Santa Elena are more likely the manifestation of the deranged imagination of Adolfo Constanzo, who was charismatic enough to draw other unstable people to his side.

One of those people was, of course, Elio Hernandez. Elio, who has confessed to being involved in thirteen murders, says it was Sara Aldrete who talked him into joining the cult. He describes the moment when Constanzo initiated him into the cult:

"I was blindfolded and stripped and laid facedown on the floor of the wooden shack at the ranch. I became scared, but I didn't say anything. The Godfather encouraged me. Later I heard something like maracas and other voices that were saying strange words, something like 'egguala.' [Possibly Elio heard "Elegguá." In Santeria, Elegguá is the messenger of the gods. He stands behind doors and opens or closes the way to opportunity.] I think that demons were being invoked because they were naming various people, but they weren't naming anyone who was there, or my friends. They gave me a cup to drink, something like hot vinegar laced with cane liquor. Then I felt smoke in my windpipe, back, and face. I faintly heard voices. Later, my shoulders felt . . . felt like they were marking me. Cuts were made on my shoulder, my back, and my chest. I realized I was bleeding because I tried to scream, but the bandage smothered them. I sweat quite a bit. I felt like I had a fever. I was given two goats and two roosters to sacrifice.

"I left the house and the Godfather told me that everything was all right. From now on I was to be a priest, but the bosses were him, Sara, and Mario. [Mario Fabio-Torres, a cult member in Mexico City who is still at large.] Then I'd be next."

Palo Mayombe is a secret religion and we will

never know everything that went on. However, from the statements that some of the cultists made before they went silent on the advice of lawyers, and from interviews with police officials and families of the victims, we have a sufficiently vivid history of the murders at Matamoros.

What follows is a listing of all the murders that, allegedly, are associated with Adolfo Constanzo or his followers.

In Mexico City

Jose de Jesús Gonzalez-Rolono

Gonzalez, age unknown, was a Mexico City native who owned FM y Associados. The company was ostensibly a manufacturer of fire extinguishers, but allegedly was a front for a cocaine-processing laboratory.

On May 1, 1987, Mexican investigators, following up on a missing person's report, went to FM y Associados. There they found chicken eggs, garlic, cigars, and bottles of cane liquor. While such items were common in homes, they struck the detectives as odd in a factory. One detective recognized them as items that are used in a black mass.

The black mass noted here, and the one in which the transvestite Claudia, was murdered, lends credence to the idea that Constanzo was involved in what might legitimately be called Satanism. The black mass is a perversion of the Catholic mass, created by satanists to express their hostility toward Christianity. Some scholars believe it dates back to the fourteenth century. Others say it is a "literary creation" going back no further than the eighteenth century.

In his book *Satan Wants You* (Mysterious Press, 1988), Arthur Lyons describes the black mass:

"In the more publicized variety of Black Mass, the Catholic missal is read backward in Latin, or, more commonly, with parts excluded, and with word substitution, such as "Satan" for "God" and "evil" for "good." The altar is either a naked woman or a coffin, and all the religious artifacts, including the ritual chamber, are black. The priests wear black robes, usually with cowls. Frequently there are substitutions for the consecrated wine . . . sometimes human urine. The host is usually a holy sacrament that has been stolen from a church, but sometimes it is made of some obnoxious substance, such as dried feces, which is either eaten or smeared on the face. The significance of these sacramental materials lies in the fact that they are bodily products, as opposed to spiritual, and, as such, are pleasing to Satan, who is a carnal deity."

The factory, on Calle Barcelona, had allegedly received a satanic blessing. As detectives probed deeper into the mystery, they found that the supposed white chemical in the fire extinguisher was cocaine, and the viscous substance they found on the floor was human blood.

On May 6, police found the bodies of Gonzalez and Celia Campos de Klein in the Gran Canal, a major channel from which sewerage flows from the north of Mexico City. Cement weights had been tied to the bodies, but had failed to keep them submerged. The man and the woman had been blindfolded and their hands had been tied behind their backs. Both of them had been shot in the head and circular cuts were found on their torsos. During the next few days, four more bodies were found in the Gran Canal and the Zumpango River, some of them in pieces. All of them were apparently sacrificed in some sort of a black mass at the fire extinguisher company.

Celia Campos de Klein

Campos, age unknown, was a Mexico City native. She worked as a secretary at FM y Associados, and was, allegedly, the mistress of Gonzalez. Her body was found with Gonzalez's corpse in the Gran Canal.

Federico de la Vega-Lostolot (also known as El Titi)

De la Vega, twenty-four, was allegedly an informer for the federales. His body was found in the Zumpango.

Gabriela Mondragon-Vargas

Mondragon was seventeen years old. She was a housemaid and allegedly the mistress of de la Vega. Her body was found in the Zumpango.

Unidentified bodies

Also, there were two unidentified males among the bodies taken from the Zumpango.

* * *

While it's never been proved that Constanzo was involved in the massacre at the fire extinguisher factory, there are strong indications.

Omar Francisco Orea Ochoa, a student at the National University in Mexico City, was a young lover of Constanzo's and occasional participant in sexual "triples" with El Padrino and Martin Quintana. Orea, who was apparently third in command of the Mexico City cult, says that, though he was not invited to participate in the black mass on Calle Barcelona, he heard something about Constanzo's officiating at it. Mexican police, after studying the details of the ritual and the condition of the bodies, are inclined to agree.

Ramon Paz-Esquivel (also known as Edgar, and as Claudia Yvette)

Claudia, thirty-nine, was a homosexual and a transvestite. Omar Orea Ochoa confesses to being at a black mass where Claudia was killed by Constanzo and cut into twenty-one pieces.

On July 2, 1988, the pieces of Claudia's body were found in four plastic bags that had been thrown into an empty parking lot.

The alleged motive for the murder was that Claudia lived in a building owned by one of Constanzo's cult members who was trying, unsuccessfully, to evict Claudia. The alleged cult member, Jorge Moran, is said to have contracted Constanzo to solve the problem.

The Calzada Family

The Calzadas were a drug-trafficking family. A

year or so before the Matamoros discovery, nine members of the family were killed on Calle Barcelona in Mexico City and thrown into the Tula River.

After the Mexico City shootout, members of Constanzo's cult reportedly admitted that Constanzo, Martin Quintana, and suspected cult member Salvador Vidal Garcia killed the Calzadas. They allegedly did so because the Calzadas had evidence of police involvement in drug trafficking (and apparently were going to reveal it or use it for blackmail). Vidal Garcia was a Mexico City federal police agent and chief of his local unit. He was also, allegedly, a high priest in the Constanzo cult. After Vidal Garcia was arrested for the murders in June, Juan Benitez told the press, "The arrest of one of our own does not make me popular, but one does what one has to do. There were another six agents involved, but we have no proof at this time to bring charges." By August of 1989, Vidal Garcia had not been tried.

In Matamoros

Lauro Martinez Mazip

In the early-morning hours of July 23, 1988, Lauro Martinez, the son of a prominent Matamoros businessman, was shot and killed, along with a twenty-two-year-old companion at Los Sombreros bar on the Avenido Obregon. (The same bar that Mark and his friends went to when they first got to Matamoros on Monday.) Police believe that the gunman on those killings was Alvaro de Leon, El Duby, and that Constanzo might have been behind the killings. That is how the story is generally reported.

El Duby himself tells the story differently.

"I joined the sect and was *rayado* (marked or tattooed) as part of my initiation to protect me from vengeance because of the murder I did at Los Sombreros. I got into an argument with Lauro and his cousin Lizandro. They followed me out of the tavern. Outside I ran into Carlos Garcia, a friend of mine. The other two shot Garcia. I had a gun so I fired at them. [Lizandro was wounded.] I thought their relatives might kill me, that's why I joined the sect."

El Duby has confessed to other killings, but he says he was always frightened of Constanzo. At one point, he says, Constanzo ordered him to cut the legs off a victim "so you won't be so scared all the time."

At Rancho Santa Elena

Saul Sauceda Galvan

It is believed that the series of events leading up to the death of Sauceda began on July 23 when El Duby shot to death Lauro Martinez in front of Los Sombreros.

It seems that the twenty-two-year-old Sauceda, who was then a policeman but later left the force, took an interest in the murders and stalked El Duby.

By April 1, 1989, Sauceda was no longer a police officer. He was running an errand for his boss, who ran an auto parts and repair shop, when he disappeared.

One theory has it that Sauceda was taken by the cult because of his suspicions about El Duby.

Juan Benitez has said that Sauceda was killed because "he was present at the death of Carlos de la Llata, and for fear that he would denounce them, they kidnapped and tortured him to death." Carlos de la Llata was, according to Benitez, a Matamoros cocaine dealer.

Sauceda's autopsy showed signs that he had been tortured with razor blades and also stabbed. Possibly Sauceda was one of the victims that Elio was talking about when, at the April 12 press conference, he said, "the boys would just stab at their bodies, but they were already dead."

Sauceda's body was identified by an X ray of a toe on his left foot that had once been broken. Afterward, Sauceda's father, Samuel, a fifty-eight-year-old fisherman, said that the only vengeance he desired was what the courts would decide. "The courts should be complied with," he said. "I can't say that I'd like the killers dead. Only God decides on death."

Sauceda's father also speculated that gang members might have had a grudge against young Sauceda from his days as a cop. "We didn't know the gang members," he said. "He knew them. David Serna was a schoolmate of his. They knew each other since primary school. They were in the same class."

Sauceda's mother, Marta, said her son "had a very strong character" and "got angry easily." Adrian Mejia, who worked with Sauceda at the auto parts shop, said he was "a good kid."

"He had a good sense of humor and he worked hard," Mejia said. "It's hard enough when someone dies in an accident, but this was worse than any accident."

José Luis García de Luna

After coming home from school on February 25, José, fourteen years old, had a snack and then ran off to his afternoon job of feeding cows on the Rancho Villa Hermosa, which was about a mile away from his own family's farm, and not far from the Rancho Santa Elena.

On the way out he asked his father, who was headed into town, to pick up some music cassettes.

"I'll be back at five," he called to his mother, Ericada, as he left that day.

When José didn't come home that night, his parents knew that something was terribly wrong.

"He was a very obedient boy," his mother says. "When he didn't come home, we knew someone must have taken him. It wasn't like him to stay out like that. He never strayed far from the ranch. He had no vices, few friends. He was my youngest and always stayed around the house to help me."

At some point during the day, probably on the way home from his job, young José discovered that his goat was missing. He began walking along the back roads, calling for it.

During the time that José was searching for his

goat, the cultists had gathered in the shack and were about to make a human sacrifice. However, the man they were about to kill had somehow concealed a gun. He pulled out the gun, and Elio was forced to shoot him to death before he could ritually be murdered. This left the group without a sacrifice, so Elio sent a few of the boys out with orders to kidnap the first person they saw.

It happened to be José. The men put a gunnysack over José's head and brought him back to the shack. Elio sacrificed the boy by chopping his head off, without even removing the sack. The cultists then took out the boy's lungs and his brain, which, presumably, were cooked in the nganga.

It wasn't until they buried the boy that Elio recognized José's gray and green football shirt and realized that he had decapitated his own cousin.

After the bodies were discovered, José's family went to the Glayoso Funeral Home in Matamoros, where some of the bodies were displayed. José's twenty-five-year-old sister, Rosalita, was given the task of looking behind the curtain to identify the youngest of her brothers.

"He had no head," she says. "It was chopped off, by his side. But I knew it was him by the shirt he was wearing. It was gray and green. He always liked sports, especially baseball and football."

Later Ericada Garcia, weeping, talked to a reporter for the *Brownsville Herald*. "If it weren't for the Kilroy boy," she said, "none of the other men, including my son, would ever have been found."

When José's brother Frederico was asked about

the family connection to Elio Hernandez Rivera, he said there had been domestic problems between those two branches of the family. "We never had anything to do with him," Frederico said. He added that his family had no idea about the cult activities.

"We didn't notice anything different about him. The only way you'd know he did these horrible things is because he opened his mouth and said he did them."

When it came out in the local papers that José's family couldn't even afford to buy a body bag for him, students at Rio Grande High School collected $300 and sent it to the family.

"We're going to get to fix up the grave and put a name on the tombstone," José's father, Isidoro, later told Tom Ragan of the *Brownsville Herald*. "I still can't believe this happened to us. These types of things only happen in television shows, and now look."

The father also said that since José's death no one in the family would leave the house alone. "If we ever go out, we go out together," he told Ragan.

"I'm afraid for my children, not for me," José's mother said. "I've already lived my life. I had five sons, now I only have four."

Gilberto Garza Sosa

Garza, forty years old, was a former railway policeman who was allegedly involved in narcotics trafficking. The Mexican police say he had connections to a narcotics ring that smuggled drugs into the U.S. He was, reportedly, tortured and then murdered in revenge for a drug deal that went bad. He lived in Brownsville. The autopsy on Garza revealed that he died from hemorrhaging after suffering several blows to the body. Also, the bones in his throat were broken.

Sara Aldrete is alleged to have lured Garza into the hands of kidnappers, according to Mexican and American police. In Texas a warrant was issued, accusing Aldrete of aggravated kidnapping. According to Jack Douglas and Andrew Kirtzman, writing in the *Houston Post,* investigators said, "Using her beauty, Aldrete preyed on a victim who was killed sometime after University of Texas student Mark Kilroy was slain."

"She helped lure him into a situation where he could be kidnapped," said one Cameron County deputy.

Douglas and Kirtzman also write:

"Sara Aldrete had also been seen numerous times at the sacrificial 'slaughterhouse' on a ranch twenty miles west of here, U.S. Customs Agent Oran Neck, Jr., said. As victims would be executed and dismembered, Aldrete would stand alongside Adolfo de Jesús Constanzo, said to be the 'godfather' of the group, Neck said."

Joaquin Manzo-Rodriguez

Manzo-Rodriguez, twenty-eight, was a federal narcotics officer.

Ernesto Rivas-Diaz

Rivas-Diaz, twenty-three, was a welder from

Monterrey. Apparently he was killed so that cult members could steal three tons of marijuana that he was watching over.

Ruben Vela-Garza

Vela-Garza, thirty, was allegedly murdered for the same reason as Rivas-Diaz. His cousin says he was a "quiet-type laborer with little education who didn't talk much."

He was reported missing on February 14 and was last seen getting into a pickup truck with Florida plates. His godmother, Raymunda Nunez of Port Isabel, describes him as "a good kid who never meddled in anything."

Roberto Rodriguez

Rodriguez, twenty-nine, was a federal narcotics officer.

Esquiel Rodriguez Luna

Rodriguez, twenty-seven, was identified as a farm worker who lived in Matamoros. The reason for his murder is not known.

Jorge Valente del Fierro (also known as Pedro Gloria Gomez)

Valente, thirty-five, was a former member of the Matamoros police force and an informer for the federales. Allegedly, he was a cult member and was executed for using cocaine, which was forbidden by Constanzo.

"Constanzo does not take drugs," Benitez said.

"He drinks, but he doesn't take drugs. Not one [of the cult members] is a drug user. He killed Valente del Fierro for taking cocaine."

While it seems to be true that Constanzo did not take drugs and apparently forbade them, there might have been stronger reasons for Valente's demise. He was a former cop who was known as a *madrina*. In Mexican police jargon a *madrina* is a worker whose job is an example of what we would call featherbedding. His name is not listed on the payroll, but he runs errands for his superiors and he gets a salary. The errands typically include collecting bribes. A *madrina* is also what we would call a stool pigeon, an informant for the police. He walks a tightrope between the criminal world and the world of the police.

Valente's body was identified by a red rose tattooed on his right arm.

Mark Kilroy

Serafin Hernandez Garcia admits kidnapping Mark Kilroy.

"They told me to get a white guy," he says, "a student who was young." He says he knew that Kilroy would be used in a sacrifice. "I did it because they told me to do it," he says. "If I didn't do it, they'd probably do something to me. We were scared."

When the four gang members were arraigned in Matamoros on April 18, prosecutor Manuel Villegas repeated back to them some of the things they had allegedly admitted to after Benitez arrested them the week before. By this time the suspects had clammed up, so they did not reply when Villegas spoke.

"In the ranch you all used machine guns and stored marijuana," he said. "How about Kilroy's body? It is stated that you stopped by an alley, found him, and offered him a ride. He tried to escape, but you caught him and took him to the ranch. You called the Godfather and told him his delivery had arrived.

"You had him tied up in a warehouse where everyone met. The Godfather went in with Elio while the rest remained outside for fifteen minutes before a loud noise was heard like a coconut being split.

"[Kilroy] was facing the ground when hit with a machete, and his brain was taken out together with parts of his spinal column. He was later taken outside, buried, and guarded for four to five hours."

Villegas was referring to Elio's statement. Elio had told Benitez that Mark Kilroy had been taken to the ranch, stripped, and thrown on the floor, facedown. El Padrino, he said, had killed Kilroy with a machete blow to the head. Others cut out the heart and threw it into a kettle. The body, he said, was hung from a beam so that his blood flowed into the kettle.

Unidentified bodies
Three other male bodies found at Rancho Santa Elena have not been identified.

At the Orchard

Moise Castillo Vasquez

Castillo, fifty-two, was one of the two victims found in an orchard a few miles from the Santa Elena ranch. He was a construction worker who had lived in Houston, where he was a legal permanent resident. Castillo, the father of twelve grown children, owned an *ejido* outside of Matamoros, and in May of 1988 he drove his truck to the Mexico property, where he planned to plant sorghum.

Shortly after he arrived in Mexico he disappeared. The 1973 Ford truck he had driven to Mexico was found. It had not been robbed and his house had not been robbed. Castillo's father, Hidalgo, of Brownsville, went to Mexico to look for his son. That's when he met some children who told him they had come upon a grave while chasing rabbits. They told him there was a hand sticking above the earth.

When the Matamoros story broke, Hidalgo, thinking his son might have been one of the victims, drove to the Santa Elena ranch to see the burial ground.

"This is the work of the devil," he said when he stood in front of the shack. "I just cannot believe that something like this was happening here."

Later, Hidalgo Castillo went to the three Matamoros funeral homes where the bodies were held, but he was unable to find his son. After that he remembered the grave the children had told him about. He called the police. The bodies were found.

After Castillo's body was unearthed, his father said he had no idea who had killed his son.

"Before God, I suspect the whole world," he said, "but vengeance is powerful and it is God's. I can't condemn anybody."

"I don't know why they did it," Castillo's widow, Francisca, says. "He had friends. He had no enemies." The couple had been married for thirty-six years.

Hector de la Fuente Lozoya

De la Fuente, fifty-two, was murdered along with Castillo, and the two men were put in a common grave.

His wife, Monica, identified the body for police by the clothes he wore.

"He went out one day and said he would return," she said.

Neither man was mutilated.

Juan Benitez later told the press that the Ejido Santa Liberada, the ranch where the bodies were found, was co-owned by Elio Hernandez. He accused Jesse Hernandez, who was on the lam, of committing the crimes, but Jesse has not been indicted.

But why were Castillo and de la Fuente murdered?

On April 17, Siva Vaidhyanathan wrote about them in the *Dallas Morning News*:

"The two were not believed to have been sacrificed, as were most of the victims found last week

. . . but instead were victims of a drug deal gone bad, said Comandante Juan Benitez of the Mexican Federal Judicial Police.

" 'They were killed so their drugs could be taken,' Comandante Benitez said."

The next day, April 18, Robert Kahn wrote in the *Brownsville Herald*:

"Juan Benitez Ayala, commander of the Matamoros Federal Judicial Police, said the latest two victims, Castillo and Hector de la Fuente, may have been killed for inadvertently witnessing a drug-smuggling operation carried out by the cult at Santa Elena ranch.

"The two victims may have seen a truck carrying as much as two tons of marijuana, Benitez said. 'They [the smugglers] had to silence them, and they did,' Benitez said."

De la Fuente's wife was shocked at the charges that her husband was involved in drug smuggling.

"I can't believe it," she said. "I never suspected he had any relations with drug smugglers."

While many of the details of specific murders are not known, we do have some general information.

We do know that all of the victims at Santa Elena were male. "We don't believe in killing females," one of the gang members told Oran Neck.

According to Neck, all twelve victims at Santa Elena appear to have either been shot or bludgeoned to death with an ax or machete. But according to Frank Gibney, writing in *Newsweek,* "one man had been boiled alive, his face still etched in a scream." All of the bodies had been mutilated. According to the alleged killers, most of the mutilation was done after the victims were dead.

After the killings it was widely reported that "almost all the victims were criminals," and that most of the murders were "revenge crimes." Both assertions are debatable. And even if a victim was a criminal, his murder could have been a sacrifice to the gods. As noted from Gonzalez-Wippler, for the mayombero who is making a nganga the choice kiyumbas, (that is, the dead bodies, or the brains of the dead) are "those belonging to very violent people, especially those of criminals or the insane."

Police believe that all of the Matamoros victims were murdered between June 1988 and the discovery in April 1989. Some of Constanzo's alleged Mexico City victims were murdered before June of 1988.

We know something about the first Santa Elena victim from the statement read by the prosecutor when Elio, Serafin, David, and Sergio were arraigned:

"He was a young man [possibly Diaz] who was hitchhiking. He asked to be taken to the bus station in Matamoros," the statement says. "Instead, he was taken to the ranch where he was tied up with masking tape to be sacrificed as ordered by the Godfather.

"The Godfather and Quintana proceeded to cut his throat and drain his blood to be poured into the large kettle.

"Then Constanzo ordered that he be buried."

There is no clear record of who killed whom. Some of the suspects claim not to have murdered anybody. Others minimize their involvement.

According to George Gavito, Elio has said that only he and Constanzo committed the ritual murders.

But El Duby has recalled one sacrifice where he killed a victim with a ceremonial dagger. At another, he says, he smashed a man's head open with a machete and carved out his spine for a ceremonial necklace.

Serafin Hernandez Garcia admits to kidnapping at least five of the men who were murdered and mutilated, but says, "I didn't kill nobody." He recalls witnessing only one murder.

"There was one in the shack. The *padrino* slit his throat. About six of us stood around." Serafin says the gang watched the murder, which was done over a crude altar, by candlelight.

Elio Hernandez, describing what happened to the victims after they were dead, has said, "Some, they'd take out the hearts and put them in a kettle. Another, he hanged from a tree near the house and the blood that flowed from the body drained into the kettle."

Elio had, reportedly, laughed when he told the story.

SEVEN

The Reaction

Juan Benitez Ayala didn't like all the attention. Head up, eyes forward, he stood on the second-floor balcony of the Federal Judicial Police headquarters, where he was the commandant, and looked across the courtyard. Then he stared down at the gathered reporters—thinking, perhaps, they are here from all over the world to talk to *me*—and probably feeling uncomfortable about it.

Though he would later be described in *Texas Monthly* as a man who "pandered irresistibly to the media," people who know him describe him as a man who avoids the press.

Anthony Zavaleta, the anthropology professor at Texas Southmost College in Brownsville, says, "As I got to know Benitez, I was amazed to see that he was a person who tried to stay away from publicity. I know firsthand that he is not a publicity seeker."

The reporters, crowded into the small brick courtyard behind the building, waited anxiously

for the commandant to convene the afternoon
press conference. It was Wednesday, April 12, a
warm spring Mexican afternoon, and a breeze
swept over the stone walls of the courtyard. Benitez
inhaled deeply, perhaps feeling just a touch of
butterflies at the prospect of speaking to this assem-
blage. The sound of the reporters chattering among
themselves rose to him, and he knew that they were
surprised, even amused by what was about to
happen. Four accused murderers were about to be
presented to the reporters. Like up-and-coming
stars at some Hollywood press junket, he might
have thought, that's probably how they see it. For
Benitez it was important that this press conference
go smoothly. He certainly didn't want it to come off
like some kind of circus.

The crowd of reporters was restless, hungry for
information. Shifting their weight from foot to foot
on the hard surface of the yard, they were like
athletes waiting for the starter's bell. Pencils were
poised on notebooks. Video cameras were aimed
like weapons at the balcony. Photographers, some
of them with as many as four cameras, and all of
them with long, barrellike lenses, were angling
around the courtyard trying to claim the best spots
for photos.

There must have been three hundred journalists
in all, mostly American and Mexican, but there
were some from England, France, Switzerland, and
Holland. The big-city newspapers were there. The
wire services were there. The television stations
were there, the radio stations, the magazine writers,
the book writers.

Standing beside Benitez on the narrow balcony were the prisoners: Serafin Hernandez Garcia, Elio Hernandez Rivera, Sergio Martinez Solis, and David Serna Martinez. All of them under the age of twenty-four.

The prisoners looked so vulnerable with their hands cuffed behind their backs. They could be pushed off this balcony, and they would be helpless to stop it. All but Hernandez Rivera stood with their heads bowed, looking appropriately shamed and humiliated by this exhibition, this public acknowledgment of their wickedness. Elio, he is the most defiant one, Benitez must have thought. There had been a report earlier that Elio had challenged the commandant to shoot him. "Go ahead," he had allegedly taunted, "shoot me. Your bullets will just bounce off me. I have a magic shield."

Now Benitez would present these men to the press, and through the press, he would present them to the world.

The commandant stood for a moment, perhaps mentally rehearsing the words he would use. There had been too many rumors already. People were saying that the cultists were about to grab children from homes and schools on both sides of the border. People were saying that Adolfo Constanzo had special powers. This press conference would set the record straight.

Though the press conference of prisoners would be seen as "typically Mexican," which it was, it was not even Benitez's idea.

"When this thing first broke, George Gavito and

161

I were the only ones dealing with the press," says Oran Neck. "Benitez was kind of publicity shy. Law enforcement officers in general are kind of suspicious of the press, until they get used to working with them and find out they're just people trying to make a living. So after we had our press conference on this side in the morning, we went to Juan and asked him to have a press conference and present the prisoners. Juan was reluctant at first; he'd only been here a couple of months at the time. But we said, hey, the world needs to know this, and he agreed. So George and I took the media over in a caravan."

Benitez might have been reluctant because he knew that it was difficult for the foreign reporters, especially the Americans, even to comprehend how such a press conference could be held. Certainly the Americans had had a press conference of their own. The American lawmen had even suggested this one. But in Mexico things were done differently, and Benitez knew that, to an American, a press conference presenting prisoners who would confess their crimes would be outrageous. Americans would wonder, how could the courts ever find an unbiased jury?

If Benitez was asked that, he would have to explain that Mexico was different. "In Mexico there is no jury," he would have to explain. "The judge will gather material, listen to witnesses, and render a decision." He would tell them that publicity in Mexico would not hurt a defendant's case.

It was going to be a challenge, Benitez must have

thought now, to explain Mexican law to Americans. Sometimes it probably seemed as if Mexicans didn't even know the law; already his countrymen were calling for the death penalty for the Matamoros cultists, even though Mexico has no death penalty. And that's not all he would have to explain to the Americans. The *brujería*. The magic, they would want to know about the magic.

Now, as he stood on the balcony, waiting for the last few reporters to be led into the courtyard, Benitez might have wondered how best to explain *brujería* to his audience. Certainly the American reporters would ask about the white candles in his office, the strings of garlic and peppers. He could explain that these were there to ward off evil. "You have to understand about Mexico," he could say. "Black magic is a part of our culture." He could tell them about the ancient Aztecs. No, he might have thought, not the ancient Aztecs. There had been confusion already, people saying that Constanzo practiced Aztec rituals, when his rituals were really African. Tell them about something more . . . contemporary, he might have thought. If he wanted to explain everything just right, so that they would not make Mexicans look foolish, he could tell the journalists that Mexicans were not so different from Americans.

He could tell them about the herbs, the potions, and the magic pouches that are as easy to find in the marketplaces of Mexico as a lucky rabbit's foot or pair of dice would be in the U.S.A. He could tell them about the shamans all over Mexico who cast spells and undo them for a small fee; they are as common as palm readers and psychics are in the U.S.A., he could say.

Once the conference began, Benitez presented the prisoners one by one to the ladies and gentlemen of the press. And they each in turn took their place at the front of the balcony and answered questions that were shouted at them in Spanish and English.

Elio Hernandez, defiantly, stood on the balcony and told reporters that he had been ordained as an executioner priest by Constanzo.

"I did torture a person," he told the reporters, "but the other tortures were done after the people were dead. The boys would just stab at their bodies, but they were already dead."

Elio also had a complaint about the press.

"People in the press have been saying that we drank blood and ate dead bodies, and that is a lie, that is not so."

Oran Neck agrees. "We have not found any evidence of blood-drinking or cannibalism," he says.

"Did you kill two of the men?" a reporter shouted to Elio.

"I haven't denied killing them," Elio said. "El Padrino took them inside the shack at the ranch and he told me to come in. When I came in, he said, 'Shoot them,' so I shot them."

Elio also admitting chopping the head off of one victim, his cousin.

"But why did you follow the Cuban's orders?"

was the follow-up. There was, of course, a high level of interest in Constanzo. By this time El Padrino had fled the area, along with Sara Aldrete and two other cult members. Police all over North and South America were looking for them, and already calls were coming in from people everywhere who claimed to have seen Constanzo or Sara.

"For protection," Elio said. "The Godfather told us that if we did it, bullets couldn't harm us. But it didn't serve its purpose."

"Do you regret it now?" one Mexican reporter asked.

"Yes," he said, "but it is too late now."

There were questions about Kilroy, and Elio told them that Constanzo had killed Kilroy, had split his head open with a machete.

Elio also said that two of the victims were killed "for vengeance."

Benitez stepped forward. "The scars," he said, "show them the scars." He opened Elio's shirt and pulled it down over Elio's shoulders to reveal for the reporters and the TV cameras the V-shaped marks that had been branded on Elio's arms and chest. Benitez told the reporters that the scars marked Elio as a designated murderer.

When reporters asked Elio about his split lip and the bloodstain on his sleeve, he laughed. "I punched myself," he said.

Serna and Martinez had less to say. Serna told the group that he had helped to kidnap Kilroy.

"After we took him away, Kilroy fled from us somewhere near Del Prado Hotel, but we caught him," Serna said. "Kilroy was blindfolded most of the day and he was killed about three P.M. the same day he was abducted."

Martinez talked about digging graves for the victims at El Padrino's orders. "I'm guilty," he said, but then added cryptically, "It was the thing to do."

The reporters were most anxious, perhaps, to hear from Serafin Hernandez Garcia, the American college student.

Serafin told the reporters that he had watched over marijuana shipments at the ranch, but he said, "I never killed nobody and I never crossed no drugs across the border."

He also said that the cult was "a witchcraft religion. I don't know anything about it."

"What about Kilroy?" a woman asked. "Did you kidnap Mark Kilroy?"

"Yes."

"Why?"

"They told me to get a white guy, a student who was young. I knew Kilroy would be killed and used in a sacrifice. I did it because they told me to do it. If I didn't do it, they would do something to me. We were all afraid."

Serafin's "they" presumably refers to Constanzo and Elio, who led the gang and did the killing. His "we" would be himself, Martinez, Serna, and other gang members who were still at large.

Serafin told the reporters how he had sat in the pickup truck at two A.M. on March 14 and picked Mark Kilroy at random. He said he had called to

Kilroy, "Hey, do you need a ride?" and when Kilroy had walked over, they had grabbed him. "I got into the truck and we took him away." He said that Kilroy was killed about twelve hours later. "I did not kill him," he said. "The one who killed him was our *padrino*. He did it with a machete, with a single blow from a machete—I didn't see it."

Serafin was asked if he had anything to say to other young people.

He answered, "I would tell my classmates don't do it, don't get into drugs. You don't know what you're going to get into, you don't know what's going to happen."

That was quite an understatement. But the understatement of the day came later from Domingo Reyes, the caretaker. Reyes had been booked as a material witness, but had not been charged with any murders, and he was free to go home. But he was staying at the police station, he told reporters, because he was afraid other gang members would kill him.

"I didn't know anything about this," he said. "I thought they were good people, because they presented themselves as good persons, but now I don't think so."

Reyes also told reporters that he was not allowed to talk to Kilroy, who was sitting in a hammock next to the main house and was guarded by heavily armed gang members.

Even before this press conference, the Matamoros killings were on everybody's mind. The story had made front-page news everywhere. CBS led with it. *Newsweek, U.S. News and World Report, USA Today,* and *People* also gave it a big play. Oprah did a show. Geraldo did a show. "Inside Edition" did a show. "20/20" covered it, and "America's Most Wanted," which had done a segment on Mark Kilroy when he was missing, did a follow-up.

The main story, streaking through the continent like an electric current, touched many lives. It became the parent for dozens of smaller, often anecdotal stories, and most of them involved Satanism.

The rituals had been defined in the press variously as Palo Mayombe, Santeria, voodoo, witchcraft, Cuban black magic, and Satanism. And for each label there was some indignant group or individual who called the press to explain, "Well, no, you see, this isn't really Palo Mayombe," or witchcraft or whatever, because such and such and such.

In Massachusetts, Laurie Cabot, head of the Witches League for Self-awareness, was outraged that Sara Aldrete was being called a "witch" in the press, and that the term "witchcraft" was being used to describe the murders in Mexico.

"We are not satanists, we do not do black magic or any evil magic," Ms. Cabot said, speaking for the 900-member group, which is a kind of anti-defamation league for witches.

Ms. Cabot, a Kiwanis Club member, who had been named the official witch of Salem, Massachusetts, in 1975 by Governor Dukakis, wanted to remind the press that Wicca was a legally recognized and peacefully conducted religion. It was, she said, a natural religion that used astrology, astronomy, and psychic healing, as well as potions and spells. "But always for good," she said. "Never for bad."

In Florida, where 60,000 people, mostly Cuban Americans, practice Santeria, Ernesto Pichardo, the santero priest in Hialeah's Church of the Lukumi Babalu-Ayé, tried to offset the anti-Santeria hysteria by educating the press about his religion.

Fair enough. Nobody likes to have the label "crazed cult killers" hung on them. But something fearsome had gone on down there. To call it Santeria was no less correct than to call it Satanism, and that was the term getting the most play. The Matamoros rituals had nothing to do with the Church of Satan, certainly, and except for the alleged black masses in Mexico City, there is no indication that Constanzo was practicing Satanism at all. However, the Matamoros rituals were definitely satanic in the sense that they were wicked, diabolical. Right or wrong, when the public talked about the trouble in Matamoros, they talked about Santeria, and more often, they talked of Satanism.

In Brownsville, where the *Brownsville Herald* did a credible job covering the story, people who had stored up some venom for the media found an easy target: Geraldo Rivera.

Rivera taped a show about the murders, with himself in New York and Texas reporter Bob Salter live in Brownsville with an audience of local citizens. Long before the show was televised, Geraldo's name in Brownsville was mud. Everybody wants to be a producer, and most of the people who participated in the show thought it could have been done differently. Some people in Brownsville accused Geraldo of sensationalism, though it would be hard to imagine how you could do a show about thirteen people being ritualistically tortured, butchered, and cooked by devil-worshiping drug smugglers without sensationalizing it.

Texas Attorney General Jim Mattox, who was on the Geraldo show, stirred his own tempest of controversy. Texas governor Bill Clements accused Mattox of casting himself into the drama simply to make political hay of it. Mattox responded by writing letters to all the big-city papers in Texas, explains that he was just doing his job, and that he had been invited to the area by local lawmen.

Rumors spread like a flu virus through south Texas schools. In Pharr, Texas, the day after the bodies were dug up, a schoolboy heard over a Mexican radio station that students were being kidnapped by cultists. He spread the word. Parents rushed to the school to pull their kids out early. The next day the panic spread to other schools in the area. By the third day many schools had more kids out than in.

In Hemphill, on the Texas-Louisiana border, kids became hysterical over rumors that a local student would be kidnapped and sacrificed in a cult ritual, and that several teachers were members of a satanic cult. This rumor gained more credibility than others, perhaps, because the recent shooting of a local woman and the arrest of her fourteen-year-old son was said to be cult-related.

On April 14, a woman identifying herself as Sara Aldrete called federales headquarters and said if her friends were not freed, she would begin kidnapping and murdering children. Later, it was announced that the call was placed by a madwoman in a Houston psychiatric ward.

All over the country, counselors stood in classrooms, and psychiatrists talked on radio. Let your kids talk about the murders, they urged. Watch for drastic mood changes, they said. Watch for changes in friendship groups, signs of drug involvement. These, they said, were all possible indicators of cult activities. In some school systems the peace symbol was banned on the grounds that it was also a satanic symbol. Everywhere, parents kept a closer watch on their children.

At Our Lady of Refuge, a cathedral that overlooks Matamoros's main plaza, the Reverend Ruperto Espinoza noticed a big jump in church attendance.

"Now people are saying, yes, evil exists," he said.

In Mexico City, Mexican president Carlos Salinas de Gortari, who had already built a pretty good reputation as a drug fighter, promised to "make life impossible for drug traffickers." Though skeptics thought the war was unwinnable in a country where drugs have been part of the economy for centuries, there were signs that the Matamoros incident had ripped away the veil of public apathy. More and more, it seemed, distressed Mexicans saw their country spiraling downward toward that shameful fate of becoming another Colombia.

In Houston, radio station KZFX hired painters to remove the word "voodoo" from a billboard promoting its "voodoo Wednesday" skit. "We didn't want to be associated with it, out of consideration to the Kilroy family," a spokesman explained.

In video rental shops everywhere, clerks noticed a run on the film *The Believers*. When news stories reported that the movie had been used as a recruiting film by Constanzo's young cult members, the stores had thousands of calls for the film. Some Brownsville stores, not wanting to cash in on the tragedy, pulled the movie from their shelves.

In Washington, Representative Solomon Ortiz of Corpus Christi called for a congressional investigation of drug abuse and occult worship.

In Texas, Harlingen representative Larry Warner filed a bill that would allow Texas to prosecute the killers of Mark Kilroy even though the killing took place in Mexico.

"If one of our citizens gets murdered abroad, the people back in Texas are the ones who have the right to avenge the victim," Warner said. On May 4, 1989, the Criminal Jurisprudence Committee of the Texas legislature voted unanimously to send the bill to the full house.

Throughout the Southwest a mournful procession of people poured into Matamoros. The reports of unidentified bodies turned the city into a kind of mecca for those whose mates had vanished, whose children had run away. Thousands of people went to the funeral homes to view the twisted remains. Some hoped to find their loved one's body and end what one man called "the awful pain of not knowing." Others perhaps sought renewed hope in seeing that none of the bodies were familiar.

Their stories are poignant.

There was the Charleston, South Carolina, man who thought his stepson, who had been missing for eight months, might be a victim. "One day Jeff left a note that said, 'I'm going to disappear for a while if any of my friends call,'" the Charleston man explained. He said that his stepson had taken "a turn for the weird" because of the strange music he listened to and possible drug use.

There was the mother of Ruben Vela-Garza. He was the thirty-year-old field-worker from La Pesca whose body was the last to be identified. After identifying the remains, his mother, elderly and fragile, left the funeral home with tears in her eyes and a handkerchief over her mouth. There was a look of horror and disbelief on her face.

"No puede ser," she said. It cannot be.

Not long after the discovery, the cult killings worked their way up the charts in the form of a hit song called "Tragedy in Matamoros." The song, sung by the group Suspiros de Salamanca (Sighs of Salamanca), was a traditional ballad played in waltz time with guitars and accordion. It became a hit in Mexico and among Mexican-Americans in Houston, Dallas, and San Antonio, as well as in the

Rio Grande Valley. Here is a translation of the lyrics:

There the devil did fail them satanic
   murderers.
They say Sarita Aldrete
And that Cuban "El Padrino"
Are the main ones responsible
For everything that has happened.
In Brownsville and Matamoros
They all started trembling
Because that satanic gang,
They are not afraid to kill.
That's how they prayed to the devil,
In order to triumph in all that they do.
The parents were very worried
About their beloved son.
That young American,
Well, he had been lost
On the fourteenth of March
While he was out with some friends.
They say that some federales,
They caught a snitch.
"We will protect you.
Give us some good information."
"The Santa Elena ranch,
It looks like a cemetery there."
Now I say good good-bye from here
From Rancho Santa Elena.
Here they found the gringo
Dead with another dozen.
For that satanic gang,
Black will be their sentence.

Perhaps the most enduring image to follow the deaths in Matamoros was that of the Kilroy family saying their good-byes to Brownsville and going home without their son.

Mrs. Kilroy talked to reporters. She thanked them for keeping Mark in the public eye and helping to find him. The messages of sympathy from the public had been, she said, "overwhelming."

"Mark," Mrs. Kilroy said, "is with our Lord. We don't have to worry about him anymore. I know he's hearing my words now and I know he's telling me, 'Mom, everything is okay.'"

She told the reporters she had no malice toward the men who killed her son. "I think they must be possessed by the devil," she said. "That can be the only explanation for what they did. I pray for them all. They should ask forgiveness of Mark and one day they can apologize to him."

Mark's brother, Keith, told the reporters, "Mark was always there when I needed him. I listened to him, and I will keep on listening to him."

When Jim Kilroy was asked what he would say to his son's murderers, he replied, "I would just tell them they ought to ask for forgiveness and mercy from God because the devil won't do it for them."

While the Kilroys expressed no hatred, no anger with the killers, they were clearly a family with a new mission in life.

"Drugs killed my son," Jim Kilroy said. "He didn't take drugs, but drugs killed him. When people say a little marijuana doesn't hurt anybody, they're wrong, it killed my son."

Kilroy said he would push for legislation for drug testing in the schools and tougher sentences.

Mark Kilroy's body was cremated. A memorial service was held in Brownsville. Then the Kilroys went home.

At Santa Fe High School two dozen of Mark's friends got together and watched home movies of basketball games and a "senior follies" that he had taken part in.

One of his friends, Suzanne Harvel, said, "Everyone wanted to get together and remember Mark the way he was."

And in Georgetown, Texas, Clemmie Schroeder, a woman described as "spiritual adviser" to death-row inmate Henry Lee Lucas, sent a map to the attorney general's office. Lucas, who had been on death row for five years, had once confessed to murdering 360 people, but later retracted his confessions, saying he had only murdered three, including his mother. The map, allegedly drawn by Lucas in 1985 while he was in prison, reportedly highlighted several locations where drug smuggling, kidnapping, and ritual murder were occurring in Mexico.

"Henry told me there were a lot of different cults in Mexico who were involved in satanic worship and everything," Schroeder told the *Brownsville Herald*. "I found the map and realized he had marked this cult and drug ring near Brownsville."

Attorney General Jim Mattox was not available for comment about the map, but a spokesperson for him said, "At this point, with the bizarre things that have been discovered down there, you really can't discount anything totally." No action was ever taken in response to the map.

In Brownsville, Tony Zavaleta was concerned that no visual record was being made of the Matamoros shack. And so on Saturday, April 22, Zavaleta packed his video camera into his car and drove from his home in Brownsville across the International Bridge to Matamoros and out to Rancho Santa Elena.

"I went for documentation," he says. "I wanted to have a record of what was there. I knew things were being carried off or disturbed or moved around. But when I went home Saturday night and viewed my videotape, I recognized that I didn't have what I wanted. I had glossed over some things; I had not held shots long enough for me to really look at something and study it."

So Zavaleta went back on Sunday to videotape once more, and he got a lot more than he had expected.

"I had no idea that the federales were going to show up. But up drives five Blazers. Out jump all these guys with automatic weapons, and they were jumpy as hell. I mean these guys were *jumpy*. These guys are believers and they're looking around and they don't know what's going to happen. They don't know if armies from the devil are going to come and wipe them out. They were there to burn Constanzo's shack. But they're not going to just burn it, they're going to *ritually* burn it. They brought the *curandero* with them, and he did all kinds of ritual cleansings, the *limpia* again, and things that needed to be done. He had his chanting and his incantations and he went around the thing and he sprinkled water and oil and he did what he had to do. He had an assistant. His assistant was a young boy and he had a cardboard box, and that little boy kept that cardboard box over on the side of the area and he guarded that box. And every now and then the healer would go over and look in the box.

"What was in the box was a white dove, a live white dove, and the theory was, if the dove dies, then we're in deep shit because that means evil has won in the end. If the dove lives, we won and evil has been vanquished. There was a battle to the death going on between good and evil. The commandante was the champion of good, and Constanzo was the champion of evil. The commandante burned the shack so that Constanzo would know, we burned your building, we burned your nganga, we destroyed your source of power, the nganga, the cauldron, therefore we have neutered you. And I'm happy to tell you the dove lived."

Zavaleta acknowledges that the idea of lawmen burning the scene of a crime and possibly evidence long before a trial is difficult for the American mind to understand.

"Certainly," he says, "it's totally out of context for us. But for them it was the culturally appropriate thing to do. If you look at any religious text on witchcraft, you'll see that fire is the ultimate purifier. To absolutely conclude this evil episode they had to burn that shack. It was like an exorcism. They were sending Constanzo a message. It would be a psychic or spiritual blow to him to know that that kettle and all its evil contents, the source of his power, in the belief system of Palo Mayombe, had been destroyed."

EIGHT

The Nightmare

A few days before the Mexican police discovered the bodies of Mark Kilroy and the others, a man by the name of John Westcott, who lives in one of those picturesque New England towns you see on Christmas cards, had a talk with his teenaged son about Satanism.

"They're doing it over by the post road," the son said, referring to an area a few miles west of town where there were few houses and acres of woods.

"How do you know?"

"I heard about it," the son said. "One of the people who lives out there saw six kids go into the woods at night. They were wearing sheets, you know, like the Ku Klux Klan or something. The guy saw candles burning and he heard chanting. The police went in there the next day and they found cats that had been murdered and cut open. They took pictures and everything."

"Why haven't I heard about this?" Westcott asked.

"They're keeping it secret," the son said. "They don't want people to know there are Satanists in this town."

At eight o'clock that night Westcott drove out to the area his son had described. The woods were divided by a long and bumpy road that had once carried carriage traffic across the state. Now it is never driven on, except by teenagers who go out there to neck. As Westcott drove, the road became less smooth and more narrow, and after a few miles it came to a dead end. He got out of his car and walked into a clearing in the woods, an area where some years back trees had been cut down and stumps hauled away for some intended subdivision that never came to be. This is where the alleged satanic rituals had taken place, and Westcott walked cautiously across the area, carrying his flashlight in case darkness came too soon.

Just beyond the clearing he came to a small circle of trees, where fieldstones had been arranged into a crude altar. On one tree a pentagram had been drawn with green spray paint. The pentagram, an ancient symbol of good used by white magicians has been adopted, in its inverted form, as a symbol of evil by satanists. Scattered about the area where John Westcott stood were the melted remains of burnt candles and about a dozen empty beer cans. If any animals had been tortured and murdered, there was no evidence of it in the area now.

Just some rebellious kids acting out their annoyance with the world in a harmless way, John thought. He went home, feeling less uncomfortable than he had been. Whatever the kids had done out there, it seemed, it was no big deal.

And then a few days later he heard about the murders in Matamoros, Mexico, and he wasn't so sure.

What John Westcott found in the woods—the pentagram sprayed on the tree, the candles, the stone altar—can be found in many remote areas all over the United States and Canada. No one questions the fact that there are kids listening to heavy metal rock music that, intentionally or unintentionally, delivers satanic messages. No one questions the fact that kids are drawing satanic symbols, holding secret meetings, conducting rituals, whispering code words, even throwing sheets over their heads and chanting. That much is clear.

What is less clear is how much of this is going on, how violent does it get, how organized is it, and how worried should we be?

There's nothing new about this. Kids have always been smitten with the idea of secret ceremonies, magic symbols, and personal code words that created for them a world not violated by adults. And long before the term "heavy metal" was coined, there were those who said that rock and roll was the music of Satan and that Elvis Presley was the devil incarnate.

But in the 1980s the media spotlight has been aimed more often and more intensely at anything to which the adjective "satanic" can be attached. We have all heard many reports of pets and livestock being mutilated, children being abused at day care centers, and various felonies—especially drug dealing—being committed, all by satanist or satanic cults.

Why is a discussion of Satanism of any relevance in a book about the Matamoros cult murders? Two reasons. One is that what went on at the Rancho Santa Elena is what the public calls Satanism, even if that term is not technically correct. Secondly, Satanism and Palo Mayombe, as Constanzo practiced it, fall together under a broad and frightening category of crime that is on the rise: ritual crime. They both feed on the same mentality, they both take the most violent and grotesque forms, they both involve random murder, mutilation of bodies, and great secrecy. If there is a great satanic conspiracy out there, as some people believe, we may be in for a very large crop of Adolfo Constanzos. And even without a conspiracy, we should brace ourselves.

Writing in the *New York Times* (July 16, 1989), Wayne King describes a course in Satanism for police officers. He notes that the course convened on the day the bodies were found in Matamoros. He goes on to write, "For most Americans such incidents probably seem to be just another streak of madness running through society. And to those who have studied the subject, Satanism is a handy catchall for a range of dark beliefs. The crimes run from what might be regarded as vandalism to much more serious matters of grave robbing and ritual murder. There is no central clearinghouse for the tabulation of such offenses, so there are no hard numbers to go by.

"But there are straws in the wind, and some are disturbing."

Robert Fiallo also sees straws in the wind. "I think there is a ritual crime problem because of the way things are evolving," he says. Fiallo is the Dade County cop who teaches law enforcement agencies around the country about religious systems and how to recognize signs of ritual crime.

"There are a lot of adolescents that you might call 'dabblers,'" he says. "They are influenced by rock music and magic and drugs. Often the music has recurring themes of suicide, physical torture, abuse of women, and sexuality that is appealing to some teenagers. Let's say one or two percent of the kids go a little further, actually act out something. And let's say one or two percent of those go even further than that. Is it going to be a problem? I think so. It only takes one Ted Bundy to kill how many people?"

Ritual crime, according to Fiallo, is "crime that is committed in a ritualistic fashion and based on a system of belief. If you don't have some type of belief, then you don't have the ritual. There has to be a myth behind it, a belief behind it."

Clearly, there was a system of belief behind the murders at Matamoros. The killers believed they could appease the gods, buy protection for their dope-smuggling operation with their human sacrifices. Less clear, but just as deadly, are the beliefs behind Satanism. But Satanism is what the public knows best, and in a discussion of ritual crime, it is the logical place to start.

While there is much debate over how much of the satanic wave is true and how much is urban myth, we know that there have certainly been some shocking incidents.

Perhaps the best known is the case of Sean Sellers. Sellers was sixteen years old and living in Oklahoma City in 1986 when he committed three murders "in the name of Satan." A few years earlier he had become infatuated with the idea of Satanism. He read books about Satanism. He decided, he says, "to dedicate my life to Satan." In the high school cafeteria he drank vials of his own blood. In his room he built an altar and he wore ceremonial robes, lit candles, conducted private rituals. In an abandoned farmhouse, along with whatever kids he could get to show up, he led candlelight ceremonies. Apparently more alienated than his fellow students, Sellers stayed with Satan after the other members of his "coven" got bored with the whole thing. He combined his Satanism with heavy use of drugs and alcohol. He fell deeper and deeper into his private satanic world, and he made a pact with Satan to break all ten of the biblical commandments. When only murder was left undone, Sellers walked into a Circle-K convenience store and shot to death store clerk Robert Paul Bower "in homage to Satan." Six months after that, he committed the crime for which perhaps all of this was preparatory. He walked into his mother's bedroom and shot her and his stepfather to death in the name of Satan. Sellers was tried for the murders and sentenced to death. His current home is Oklahoma's death row, where he professes now to be a born-again Christian.

Also well documented are the misdeeds of serial killer and self-styled satanist Richard Ramirez, known as the Night Stalker. Ramirez, who has a pentagram tattooed on the palm of his hand, murdered several Californians in their homes, then mutilated their bodies and spray-painted satanic symbols on their walls.

There are other cases. But for each proven case of satanic mischief, there seem to be a dozen others that are full of holes. There are "reports of" and "alleged incidents." There are rumors, exaggerations, and outright hoaxes.

One reason that dubious accounts of satanic activity get such play is, says Arthur Lyons, that Satanism sells newspapers. In *Satan Wants You,* Lyons writes:

"There are several problems with this current rash of media accounts. Because 'Satanism' is a buzzword that captures the public's imagination and therefore sells newspapers, there is a tendency to mislabel and print such claims unskeptically. One example is the 1987 case of the Finders, in which newspapers from coast to coast carried the story that Tallahassee police had arrested two members of a "bizarre satanic cult" on felony child molestation charges. The charges were later dropped and the Finders was found to be not satanic, but a pacifistic Taoist cult. Nonetheless, most of the newspapers that originally carried the 'satanic' headlines did not bother to update developments in the story, thus perpetuating in the public's mind the growing menace."

Henry Lee Lucas, the man who allegedly drew a map showing the site of the Matamoros killings, once told the FBI that he was part of an international satanic group called the Hands of Death. He said the cult had a training camp in Florida, sacrificed animals, cut people's heads off, and drank urine and blood. Lucas also confessed that he had lured more than 360 kids to a ranch in Texas for sex and then murdered them. Authorities now believe that Lucas made all of this up to confuse lawmen and prevent them from solving the few murders that he did commit.

Television viewers have also been told about satanic murders that may or may not have occurred.

When Oprah Winfrey did a show on "Satanic Worship" in 1988, one man stood up to say he was a follower of the Satanist Church in Chicago and that at the end of one ceremony, he and others ended up murdering someone.

"It wasn't anybody I knew," he said. "And I reported it. They were stabbed seven times. It was about '80, '81. And the ritual was a witches' Sabbath, and it got out of hand, and the high priest brought out these seven daggers and they impaled him in the form of a cross with the seven daggers."

The man claimed that he subsequently had a nervous breakdown and now suffered from partial amnesia about that particular night.

"The only thing I can really remember about that

night itself is that I walked in, I got my acolyte robe on, and the next thing I remember about seeing was this guy lying on the table with seven daggers sticking out of his chest."

Nobody was ever found and no arrests were ever made.

Another guest on that same Winfrey show was Lauren Stratford, author of *Satan's Underground* (Harvest House, 1988). Ms. Stratford told the audience that she had been born illegitimately and given to a family that later got involved in Satanism. She said she was used as a breeder to have children who were later murdered in snuff films and satanic rituals. Like many of the people who claim to have been abused by satanists, Mrs. Stratford has turned to Christianity and was anxious to have the world know that. Whether or not this desire to preach Christianity inspires people to invent attention-grabbing satanic stories is difficult to say, but since Christians invented Satan, it is not surprising that as a group they would be likely to believe his work is being done.

One reason that it is difficult to get a clear picture of Satanism in America is that the waters have been considerably muddied by a good many fanatics, alarmists, and well-meaning fools.

For example, in a widely distributed pamphlet entitled "Is Satan in Your Schoolyard," published by The New Federalist, readers will learn, among other things, that there is a "Satanic plot to destroy western civilization once and for all," that the Episcopal Cathedral of St. John the Divine in

Manhattan is "one of the major centers for the spread of Satanism and Satanic Sexual Violence in North America," that the entire New Age movement is "Satanic," and that among the Satanists are Margaret Mead and Robert McNamara. And that's not all. In this pamphlet, written in part by convicted felon Lyndon Larouche, readers will also learn that Mikhail Gorbachev has a satanic symbol on his head, that the best-organized satanist forces operating in the United States include The Lucis Trust, which runs the only religious chapel in the New York headquarters of the United Nations, and that among its leading sponsors, presumably satanist or satanic puppets, are Norman Cousins, John D. Rockefeller IV, and Thomas Watson, former U.S. ambassador to Moscow. Furthermore, readers will learn that this Satanic group has "front organizations" and that among them are The World Wildlife Fund, U.K. Amnesty International, and UNICEF. Obviously, none of these claims have ever been substantiated.

To get a clearer picture of satanic activity in America it helps to divide Satanism into what might be called traditional or institutionalized Satanism, and home-grown Satanism.

The official home of institutionalized Satanism is Christianity. Specifically in the New Testament, God judges the crimes of the angel Lucifer and changes his name to Satan, the Devil, or "Evil One." Satan is banished forever, and in the Book of Matthew, chapter 25, verse 41, Jesus says that hell was created for the Devil and his angels. The irony of this is that anyone who wants to be a satanist and wants to do it right has to go to the Christians to ask them how to do it.

In *Encyclopedia Handbook of Cults in America* (Garland, 1986), Dr. J. Gordon Melton, director of the Institute for the Study of American Religion, puts it this way:

"Satanism as it now exists and has existed during the past two centuries has been a most unusual cult. It has produced almost no literature and individual groups have come and gone without connecting with previously existing Satanic groups or leaving behind any progeny. The Satanic tradition has been carried almost totally by imaginative literature of non-satanists—primarily conservative Christians, who describe the practices in vivid detail in the process of denouncing them. That is to say, the Satanic tradition has been created by generation after generation of anti-Satan writers. Sporadically, groups and individuals have tried to create groups which more or less conform to the Satanism portrayed in Christian literature."

In less abstract terms, the institutional home of Satanism in America is the Church of Satan in San Francisco. The Church of Satan was started in 1966 by Anton LeVay, a former lion tamer, stage hypnotist, mentalist, burlesque house pianist, and police photographer. LeVay, by all objective accounts, is neither a psychotic nor a sociopath. He seems to be more of a showman than anything else, and his church has welcomed to its doors such show business people as Jayne Mansfield, Sammy Davis, Jr.,

Keenan Wynn, and, it is rumored, a good many more celebrities who prefer not to have their names publicly associated with the church.

LeVay's goal, he says, is to present a set of rational beliefs while meeting man's need for ritual. When he is accused of worshiping nonexistent deities, he agrees and adds that all deities are nonexistent. Like all Satanism, LeVay's brand has a decidedly anti-Christian, antiestablishment bent.

In *Satan Wants You,* Lyons quotes LeVay:

"What are the Seven Deadly Sins? Gluttony, avarice, lust, sloth . . . they are urges every man feels at least once a day. How would you set yourself up as the most powerful institution on Earth? You first find out what every man feels at least once a day, establish that as a sin, and set yourself up as the only institution capable of pardoning that sin."

LeVay's church is a curious mixture of ritual (some of it designed by LeVay, to be based on the work of horror writers such as H. P. Lovecraft), psychodrama, theater, and just plain silliness. LeVay, it seems, is less like satanic killers than he is like the playful children who make up ritual just for the fun of it. Like the famous Hellfire clubs of the eighteenth century and other satanic clubs that were little more than excuses for sex orgies, LeVay's church seems to have slight connection to religion as we normally understand it. According to social psychologist Marcello Truzzi, "the Church of Satan is not really a sect of Christianity in the same sense as are most present and past Satanic groups."

So even though a discussion of Satanism would be incomplete without taking note of LeVay, it would seem that he is not really germane to a discussion of ritual crime. However, many would disagree. There are subscribers to the satanic conspiracy theory who say that LeVay's admonitions against hurting animals and people, and his proclaimed attempts to screen unstable people out of his church, are a fraud. Of course, he's lying, they say, that's what satanists do. LeVay, they say, is really the leader of a violent and deadly satanic circle. But their evidence is not forthcoming. LeVay has not been charged with anything. In fact, if it were not for the use of the word "Satanism" and all its variations, LeVay would probably go unnoticed, which perhaps is the point. Why call it Satanism at all? LeVay has answered that question himself in the church's newsletter *The Cloven Hoof.*

"It is most stimulating under that name," he writes, "and self-discipline and motivation are easier under stimulating conditions. It means 'the opposition' and epitomizes all symbols of noncomformity. It represents the strongest ability to turn a liability into an advantage . . . to turn alienation into exclusivity. In other words, the reason it's called 'Satanism' is because it's fun, it's accurate, and it's productive."

Though LeVay does not believe in the Satan of the New Testament, and admits that Satan is merely a symbol, he does invoke the name in the Nine Satanic Statements that can be found in his 1969 occult best-seller, *The Satanic Bible* (Avon, 1969):

1. Satan represents indulgence, instead of abstinence!

2. Satan represents vital existence, instead of spiritual pipe dreams!

3. Satan represents undefiled wisdom, instead of hypocritical self-deceit!

4. Satan represents kindness to those who deserve it, instead of love wasted on ingrates!

5. Satan represents vengeance, instead of turning the other cheek!

6. Satan represents responsibility to the responsible, instead of concern for psychic vampires.

7. Satan represents a man as just another animal, sometimes better, more often worse than those who walk on all fours, who because of his divine spiritual and intellectual development has become the most vicious animal of all.

8. Satan represents all the so-called sins, as they lead to physical or mental gratification!

9. Satan has been the best friend the church has ever had, as he has kept it in business all these years!

In his well-researched book, Lyons leaves the reader with the impression that LeVay is a magnetic personality, an intelligent man of good humor who is playing a game that is taken much more seriously by others than by himself. Lyons is certainly a lot more convincing than the satanic alarmists who seem to have nothing on LeVay but rumors. Still, while LeVay the man might be harmless, LeVay the symbol is a force to be reckoned with.

Walt Harrington, in the *Washington Post Magazine* (February 23, 1986), writes, "Anton LeVay is not a cartoon Satan. He's far less frightening than you might imagine, because he is admittedly a carnival hustler. Yet he is still terrifying, because he touches, if not the mystical darkness, then the psychological darkness . . . the hate and fear . . . in all of us. And because he, sadly, knows a haunting truth: Everybody wants to feel better than somebody."

However, the real threat of ritual crime in the name of Satan comes not from institutional Satanism, but from what we are calling home-grown, or self-styled Satanism, the festering, paranoid Sean Sellers sort of Satanism. It is the kind of Satanism in which some person or group, usually someone who feels alienated from family or society, picks up a few symbols, mixes them with some rumored ritual, adds candles and animal sacrifices, chants, and calls it Satanism, though it might not look exactly like the Satanism of the cult next door. Much of it among teenagers is inspired by the satanic words and symbols of heavy metal rock groups like Motley Crue, Black Sabbath, and Slayer. Probably most of it is harmless, unless you happen to be the neighbor's cat, and it will someday be a source of embarrassment to the adults these kids will become. The problem is those who, in Robert Fiallo's words, "take it a bit further." As we've seen in Matamoros, when a few unstable individuals get hold of a belief that allows them to do whatever they want, they can do a lot of damage.

The alleged satanic wave has spawned an entire industry of satanic sleuths who are alarmed by the ritual crimes of those who "take it a bit further." These real and self-professed experts can be found on talk shows and in high schools and colleges all over the continent. Some have no agenda except to preach Christianity. Others are simply concerned.

Ironically, while students and faculty at Texas Southmost College in Brownsville were still getting over the shock of Serafin Hernandez's and Sara Aldrete's involvement in ritual murders, the college sponsored one of these series of talks on Satanism, which had been scheduled before the bodies were discovered. Not surprisingly, the talks had to be moved to a bigger room to accommodate the large crowd that showed up.

One of the speakers at TSC was Terry Lewis, a representative of Exodus, a San Antonio group that is devoted to "counteracting cult influences, including ritualistic child abuse and animal mutilations." Lewis, who helps police departments investigate ritual crimes, subscribes to what might be called the "worst scenario" view of modern-day Satanism. Lewis, who comes across as an intelligent, reasonable, and well-informed young man, says that Satanism is organized in the U.S., and he says he knows it because he was once part of it. He says that there is a satanic group in "virtually every high school in America." He also says, "Now we have evidence that it is filtering down to the middle-school level." He implies that Anton

LeVay is doing diabolical things, that satanic cults are murdering people and hiding the bodies, and that there are teachers and child care workers all over the country who are sexually abusing children in satanic rituals.

Another satanic sleuth is Ted Gunderson, a former Los Angeles FBI bureau chief who now is a full-time cult investigator.

Appearing on the "Geraldo" show months before Mark Kilroy disappeared, Gunderson said, "One of the problems with Satanism is that it's psychological warfare. They take people, kidnap them off the street, take them out of their natural environment, their own people, their parents, their relatives, they don't care. It's in the rumor stage at this point, but I've received information from numerous sources about a ranch in Mexico where the children and some of these women are taken."

By the time Gunderson returned to appear on Geraldo's post-Matamoros show, the discussion of "Satanism" and "ritual crime" together had pretty much been legitimized. The two topics, already connected in the public mind, were now welded by a common motive: drugs.

On the show, titled "Drugs, Death and Satan," Rivera asked Gunderson, who was at the TV station in Brownsville, "Which comes first? The ritual worship, the Satanism, or the drug dealing?"

"It's hand in glove," Gunderson replied. "These aren't the first bodies, by the way. There have been other bodies. Lucas told the Texas Rangers about bodies down in Texas, as a matter of fact. We had

Leonard Lake in northern California; there were eight bodies there. As recent as March there were five bodies found in Tucson, Arizona, though not as much publicity as we are getting in the Mexican situation. But the drugs, barbiturates, amphetamines, marijuana, cocaine, heroin, all go hand in glove. This is the way they finance their operation. I did talk about the Mexican connection; there are other ranches in Mexico. And I'd like to tell you right now, the next burial ground that we will learn about will be in Mason County, Washington."

This show was taped a few days after the Matamoros bodies were found, and by this time, as various police agencies were investigating the backgrounds of Constanzo and his cohorts, it was becoming clear that they were dealing with this new wrinkle in the crime business. Though cult drug rings like Constanzo's were perhaps something new to the American public, they were not to lawmen, at least in Texas. Between 1985 and 1989 in Texas, there were 226 reported cases of cult-related crime, much of it involving drugs. In Houston, police detective Jaime Escalante has investigated, he says, "four or five" drug-related murders in which police found evidence that the killers were followers of Palo Mayombe. In February of 1987, Colombian hit men shot two rival drug dealers to death in Harris County, then chanted over the bodies before dumping them in the woods.

"They did the ritual so that the evil spirit of their victims could not harm them," Escalante says. "These same people have been linked with eleven drug-related murders in the Houston area. They are absolutely ruthless." Speaking in general about such criminals, Escalante adds, "These guys are very superstitious, many are illiterate. This has been passed on from generation to generation in South America and Caribbean countries and in Mexico, too."

(According to the experts, Santeria and Palo Mayombe are Afro-Caribbean and are not well-known or much practiced in Mexico. There, *curandismo,* with Indian and not African roots, is the folk religion.)

In Brownsville, DEA agent Armando Ramirez says, "Every arrest we make on the border, the suspect has some kind of black magic pouch on his or her person. It's about as common as driver's licenses."

All of this, of course, gave pause to lawmen who were beating the bushes to find these cult killers. Speaking in general about drug cults, Steve Baggs, a drug investigator for the Texas Department of Public Safety, put it this way: "They truly believe the leader has power over them after death. So they're not afraid of law officers or dying. That's something you have to think about."

Baggs has monitored cult criminal activity for six years, and he says the number of incidents involving drug rings is on the rise, and the biggest increase has been in 1988–89.

Vernon Parker, head of the DEA in San Antonio, says the cult trend has a strong Cuban and Colombian influence.

"They are heavily involved in black magic religion," he says. "They believe it protects them from police and rival gangs. Mixing drug dealers with black magic gives you an organization that is more loyal and willing to do whatever the cult leader says. For them, moving drugs is a spiritual act, not just a business."

Of course there is also a rise in ritual crime that is not, apparently, drug related. One such tragedy struck a Bronx, New York, community in June of 1989, two months after the Matamoros discovery. Thirteen-year-old Nilda Cartegena and fifteen-year-old Heriberto Marrero were driven to school by their uncle on June 9. They never came home, and school attendance records showed that the children never signed in. Friends and neighbors walked all over the Bronx distributing flyers with pictures of the missing kids. On June 20 the bodies of the two kids were found in plastic bags near the Whitestone Bridge. A source close to the case says that the teenagers were probably killed as part of a ritual. The victims were naked, and a chicken and a coconut were found nearby. This incident occurred barely a week after a Bronx man who had dropped out of sight was found, his body cut up in pieces and stuffed in garbage bags.

Teresita Pedraza, the sociology and anthropology professor, also tells a story that implies that drug money is not the only motivator of ritual murder:

"About a year ago I was called because there was an incident in New Jersey where a couple was found cut in half in plastic bags, floating in the bay.

There seemed to be some kind of connection to Santeria. These people, apparently, were involved in some sort of lovers' triangle, and the bodies were found with pink ribbons. Pink is the color of one particular goddess who was one of the wives of Changó, the philanderer."

Robert Fiallo is uncomfortable with the lumping together of Satanism and ritual crime. "They're apples and oranges," he says, but he does agree that ritual crime is on the rise.

"I wouldn't say it's an epidemic, but it is definitely on the rise," he says. "We're hearing about cases all over the country.

"I first got exposed to ritual crime when I was a homicide investigator in Miami," Fiallo says. "When I started working on Latin drug murders, I saw that a lot of Palo Mayombe was involved in drug trafficking. Typically, we'd go to the scene of a murder and find a shrine or an artifact or an icon. I would say that back then forty percent of the murders we looked at were Latin drug murders that had some of this religion involved in them. Conservatively, I would say that seventy percent of the Latins involved in murders had some level of belief in some of the Afro-Cuban religions.

"One theory of why is that the magical aspects of these religions is like a control mechanism. Since these people are involved in illegal activities, they don't have available to them the normal mechanisms to resolve problems. You can't very well call the police and say somebody stole ten kilograms of cocaine or somebody kidnapped and murdered my brother because they wanted two million dollars in drug money that I had, as ransom. So these perfectly legitimate religions allow them to become involved in magical rites where they feel that they can take retribution or gain protection from things. It alleviates the anguish and the anticipation. It's not something in the religion that's making the connection; it's something in the criminal mind. But, I feel that the dogma of the religion is such that it can be used for illegal or immoral purposes.

"I know one guy who came over in the Cuban exodus of the 1960s. He's a successful drug dealer, did time in prison, went through a load of money. He was initiated into Santeria in Cuba. He went back to Cuba and was initiated into Palo Mayombe. Now he says, when I need something done, I do Palo. When I need to get retribution, I perform Palo Mayombe.

"That's a guy using Palo for criminal activities. And in Matamoros I think we saw the extreme end of Palo Mayombe. In the case of Satanism, I think it's only logical that the kind of person who enjoys having sex with children and that sort of thing would be drawn to that religion because it would be a way to legitimize his feelings."

Fiallo says that much of the rise in Palo-related crime can be traced to the Mariel boat lift of 1980 when Fidel Castro added thousands of criminals and other misfits to the boatloads of Cuban emigrants bound for Florida.

Fiallo's main concerns these days are that ritual crime is being enculturated and that lawmen are not being trained to recognize religious symbolism in crime.

"What's going to happen fifteen or twenty years from now when you have a group of people in the Latin community involved in illegal drug activities, where it is considered a legitimate business enterprise and that's married to a religious system? What sociological impact are you going to have when you have people who have grown up in that environment? It's a very complex issue and we can't just sweep it under the rug. And it's not just these religions. Recently in Miami we had a man beheaded by a member of the Temple of Love. If that does not reek of ritualistic crime, I don't know what does. If you're going to analyze ritualistic crime, you need to know what a religion is. I think that we are in for a Pandora's box. The religious motivation can go just as deep as the monetary motivation. We've got to start training officers in religious systems. Right now there could be a lot of ritual crime going on that we don't know about, simply because the police didn't know what to look for."

If Adolfo Constanzo's crimes can be called "satanic" and "ritual murders," they also fit into another related category: cult murders.

Until recently cult murders, shocking as they are, have seemed to be too rare to warrant much attention or police training.

In August of 1969, when Beverly Hills police found the bodies of five people who had been murdered in the home of movie director Roman

Polanski, many people heard the phrase "cult killings" for the first time.

What police found was described by one policeman as "a bloody mess." The body of Sharon Tate, Polanski's starlet wife, who had been eight months pregnant, had a nylon rope tied around the neck. She had been stabbed sixteen times. Her friend Jay Sebring had been stabbed seven times and had also been shot. A rope had been tied around his neck, too. Another friend of Polanski's had been shot five times, stabbed more than fifty times, and bludgeoned on the head at least thirteen times. His body was found on the lawn along with the body of Abigail Folger, the coffee heiress, who had been stabbed twenty-eight times. The body of Steve Parent, an eighteen-year-old, was found in a car parked near the entry gate. He had been stabbed once and shot four times. The word "pig" had been scrawled in blood on the front door of the Polanskis' luxurious house. Polanski was in London when the murders occurred.

This was the work of the Charles Manson cult, a "family" of crazed misfits who were as loyal to Manson as Constanzo's people would later be to him.

The Manson cult would strike again before being rounded up. (Some authorities believe that the cult is responsible for as many as thirty-five unsolved murders.) Rosemary and Leno LaBianca would also fall victim to these lunatics. Rosemary LaBianca, stabbed forty-one times, was found with her hands tied behind her back with an electrical cord and a pillowcase over her face. Her husband was also found with a pillowcase over his face. He had been stabbed twenty-seven times and the word "war" had been scratched on his skin. The words "Death to the pigs" were written in blood on one wall, and "Helter Skelter" had been written on the refrigerator door.

On November 19, 1978, a decade after Manson and a decade before Constanzo, the world heard about another fanatical cult, but with a twist. They killed themselves. The cult leader was Jim Jones and the cult was called the People's Temple. On that day in November, under Jones's orders, 913 people drank Kool-Aid laced with cyanide. Many took their lethal dose voluntarily, while others were encouraged to do so by the presence of armed guards who were ordered to shoot anybody who refused.

Writing about Jones in *Mass Murder* (Plenum, 1985), Jack Levin and James Alan Fox offer these comments, which might well be applied to Adolfo Constanzo and his group:

"Jones's hold over his 'flock' was based on the emotional dependence of 'children' on their self-proclaimed father and fanatical leader who demanded that members kill their own families rather than turn on 'Dad.' Preparing his followers to accept the inevitability of their fate, he advocated mass suicide as an alternative to abandoning his deranged vision. 'I'd rather bring it all to a gallant, glorious, screaming end.' And that's exactly what he did."

It seems that Constanzo was nuts in the same

way that Jones was. El Padrino's plan, at least according to one follower, was to have all the cultists commit suicide. Like Jim Jones, he would not allow himself to be taken. Like Jim Jones, he would have his own "gallant, glorious, screaming end."

NINE

The Manhunt

The manhunt began in Matamoros and Texas as soon as the four suspects gave the names Constanzo and Aldrete to the police.

Law enforcement agencies on both sides of the border joined forces to hunt down the cult killers. From their interrogation of the four cult members in the Matamoros jail, they had come up with the names of ten more gang members. Oran Neck told the press that he believed, "There could be two or three dozen members of the drug gang, with ten or twelve involved in the killings."

George Gavito, when asked how many of the gang members he thought were involved in religious ritual and how many were just into drug dealing, answered, "About half and half."

Among those they were looking for were Adolfo Constanzo, Sara Aldrete, Ovidio Hernandez, Jesse Hernandez, Omar Orea, El Duby, Martin Quintana, and Mario Fabio Ponce-Torres. Police suspected that Ponce-Torres had been in on the kidnapping of Mark Kilroy, along with the cult suspects already in custody Serafin Hernandez, Martinez, and Serna.

Almost immediately, the FBI, the Cameron County Sheriff's Department, U.S. Customs, and the Federal Judicial Police of Mexico formed a task force. All agreed to exchange information and pursue one another's leads.

In Brownsville, Oran Neck, who had been on the case longer than anybody else, was determined to see it through. After sending information about the suspects all across the continent by telex, Neck told the press there was little need to explain the case's background to police thousands of miles away since they had already heard all about it on the news.

Almost as soon as the Matamoros story broke, calls started coming in from all over the United States. People claimed to have seen both Constanzo and Aldrete. Tips came in from Mexico, Guatemala, Jamaica, and Canada, as well as twenty-four different states. Oran Neck told reporters, "We've been inundated with leads that haven't paid off yet, but we encourage people to keep looking. Constanzo has a lot of self-control. He'll be hard to catch. But he will be caught."

Cameron County Sheriff Alex Perez, also speaking to the press, said, "Constanzo is too hot. I doubt that drug smugglers in Mexico would protect the fugitive, he's a ball of fire. Everybody is looking for him."

In Brownsville, Oran Neck was spending "twenty hours a day" on the job.

"We had calls from all over," Neck says. "People

who said they were experts in Palo Mayombe, psychics, a lot of self-styled detectives who supposedly knew about devil worship. Everybody wanted to come down here and help us investigate.

"We were talking to the press worldwide and getting out bulletins and erroneous sightings to police all over Central America and South America. We've never had as much interest in a crime as we had in this one.

"We had quite a few people here trying to track the suspects' activities and trying to ascertain whether or not they were in the local area. We tracked Constanzo's and the others' last hours here to give us some lead about where they might have gone. We found out they had been seen at the Holiday Inn in Brownsville. [Nobody seems to know who spotted the fugitives at the motel. An assistant manager at the Holiday Inn says, "We don't know. Customs called us and told us the two had been seen here."] From there we tracked them to the airport over in McAllen, where they had taken a Continental Airlines flight to Mexico City with other gang members the day before we found the bodies."

No one person has provided a clear explanation of what went on with the fugitive cult members that week, but from information gathered during interviews with Juan Benitez, Sara Aldrete, people who knew Sara at Texas Southmost, and a statement made by El Duby, we can conclude the following: Constanzo was alarmed by the federales' visit to Santa Elena on April third or fourth. He stayed away from the ranch, but ordered some of his gang to sneak into the ranch at night, remove most of the marijuana, and make a delivery on the American side of the river. By Wednesday he had told Sara Aldrete that they would be going away soon . . . "on vacation," she says. On Thursday, April 6, Sara said good-bye to her friends at Texas Southmost. On Sunday, April 9, Serafin went to Constanzo and told him the marijuana delivery had been made. Later that Sunday, when Serafin, Elio, Martinez, and Serna were arrested, Constanzo somehow found out about it, perhaps through an informer. He then gathered Sara, El Duby, and Martin Quintana, who was in Brownsville, and they bought tickets to fly from McAllen to Mexico City. The three men took one flight, and Sara, who had to wait to get a new visa, took a later flight. During the next few days Mexican police raided the homes of other suspected cult members and found that several of them had also fled from Matamoros.

"We tracked them [Constanzo, Aldrete, El Duby, and Quintana] into Mexico City, and we spent a lot of time trying to track them by airline to other places," Oran Neck says.

"The Mexican police thought they had gone to Miami. That's because Constanzo had put out the word among his associates that he and Sara were going there. But we never believed for a minute that they were in Miami."

In Miami, FBI agents and local police canvassed Constanzo's old neighborhoods but came up with nothing.

There were many other reports that Sara and other cult members were still in the south Texas area, or had returned. On April 17, for example, after Sara Aldrete was reportedly seen in La Gloria, Texas, FBI agents from McAllen and Brownsville raided three ranches where they had heard that cult activities, including animal sacrifices, had gone on. At one of the ranches they found evidence of *brujería,* but no suspects.

On that same Monday, the seventeenth, Mexican police raided Adolfo Constanzo's luxurious house just outside Mexico City in Atizapan. There they found a good deal of gay pornography, and in the secret altar behind the mirrors they found ritual paraphernalia, the sword, the robe, the so-called devil doll, and two marble altars, but no signs of sacrifice.

Police also found Constanzo's diary, wherein he ranked the members of his cult. He was the "padrino" (godfather). Orea was "palero mayor" (greatest or main palero, or follower of Palo Mayombe). Others were simply "palero." Some were "rayado" (marked with an arrow on their body) or "no rayado."

They also found a used airline ticket, along with Sara Aldrete's purse and passport, a discovery that would soon lead to widespread speculation that Constanzo had murdered Sara.

No men were arrested at the house. One neighbor told them about the young men who had been living there. "But they are gone," the neighbor said. "They left suddenly. I saw them carrying boxes out into the cars and then they all went away." (The men the neighbor saw were probably Constanzo, El Duby, Martin Quintana, and Omar Orea.)

At the house, police did arrest one woman, Maria Teresa Quintana. Quintana, an alleged priestess of the cult, was the sister of Constanzo's lover, Martin Quintana.

One officer who was assigned to guard the house told an Associated Press reporter, "It makes you feel creepy. I don't like to be in there alone."

In Houston there was also a good deal of activity. Also on Monday, April 17, federal drug agents arrested Serafin Hernandez Rivera, the father of Serafin Hernandez Garcia. Hernandez Rivera, who has never been accused of cult activity, was charged with possessing and importing drugs.

Houston was also one of the focal points in the search for Constanzo. FBI agents checked out the city's gay bars and other alleged Constanzo hangouts. El Padrino had close ties to Houston; he had been in and out of the city on drug business for years. Local lawmen thought Constanzo might be connected to a number of Houston drug cases, and they were anxious to have a chat with him.

Police believed that Constanzo was linked to a cocaine operation that they had busted on June 21, 1988. In that raid they grabbed twenty million dollars worth of cocaine from a house in northwest Houston. In the house they also found lighted candles, a crude altar, and according to Sergeant Mark Webb of the Houston police, "paperwork with the name Rivera on it."

Police think Constanzo might also have been the supplier for cocaine that was taken in two more raids that same summer.

While the police searched for suspects, the courts also went to work.

On Friday, April 21, six patrol cars full of Mexican security police escorted a van containing the Hernandez boys, Martinez, Serna, and Reyes (the caretaker), to the Matamoros courthouse. Traffic was blocked on both sides of the street. Police with shotguns surrounded the courthouse. The handcuffed prisoners were led in and made to stand before Judge Francisco Salvador Perez for arraignment.

The four cult members were charged with murder, kidnapping, selling drugs, having weapons, illegally disposing of human corpses, and posing as federal police officers to steal drugs from other dealers.

Reyes, the caretaker who had earlier been held only as material witness, was charged with complicity in the murders.

"How can you be so close to the site where people were being murdered and not say anything about it?" Juan Benitez later said to reporters. "Apparently, there were a number of shots fired, but Reyes claimed that he heard nothing."

After giving the order that the men be held for trial, Judge Salvador Perez said something that would be quite surprising in an American court: "They are now presumed responsible for the crimes and must prove their innocence."

In the days that followed, American newspaper

readers were to get a quick course in Mexican law. They learned that in Mexico there would be an "office trial" where all the arguments for or against the accused would be presented in writing for a federal judge. The defense and prosecution would file hundreds of documents, and the whole process would take at least a year. They would learn that Reyes would be allowed out on bond and the others would stay in prison; a prisoner's right to bond is determined by adding the maximum penalties for the crimes he is accused of, then dividing by two. If the total is less than five years, the suspect can place a bond. If it's more than five, he stays locked up. Americans would learn that in Mexico, where there is no death penalty, the maximum sentence the prisoners could get, no matter how many murders they were found guilty of, was fifty years. But they would also learn that in Mexico, unlike the U.S., fifty years in prison usually means fifty years in prison. Parole is rarely given.

On Tuesday, April 25, a federal U.S. grand jury in McAllen, Texas, about fifty miles west of Brownsville, handed down indictments against eleven people, including Constanzo, Aldrete, and the four cult members that Benitez had in custody. Though the murders had taken place in Mexico, the cult members were also wanted in the U.S. on a variety of drug-related charges, and the kidnapping of Gilberto Garza Sosa.

By the end of the first week in May, police were fairly certain that Constanzo, Aldrete, and the others were not in Miami, not in Houston, not in Brownsville or Matamoros. Some thought Sara was dead, others were certain that she was not. But more and more the various law enforcement agencies were coming to agree on one thing: Constanzo was in Mexico.

One man in particular who believed this was Federico Ponce-Rojas. Ponce is the regional attorney for a borough of Mexico City known as Miguel Hidalgo. A regional attorney is like a district attorney with a gun. He is an attorney, trained in the law, but he is also a law enforcement officer, with investigators under him. Ponce is responsible for the west side of Mexico City, eighty-nine square miles with four million people. It is an area that includes the official home of the president, most of the foreign embassies, the best hotels, the finest restaurants. During the month of April 1989, Ponce-Rojas became convinced that Adolfo Constanzo had nested in his territory.

Ponce-Rojas, six feet tall, slim, well dressed, bearded, is these days one of Mexico's heroes. In June 1989 he arrested Antonio Zorilla, former chief of the Federal Security Police, charged with masterminding the 1984 assassination of Manuel Buendia, a muckraking columnist who might be compared to Jack Anderson. Zorilla did not come quietly. For some hours he held Ponce-Rojas at gunpoint, threatening to kill him and then himself. The young prosecutor's grace under pressure won him wide acclaim, but he passes it off as "being part of the job."

For Ponce-Rojas, the Zorilla incident was the second well-known case he was part of in 1989. The other was Constanzo.

Ponce-Rojas is not good at sitting still. He paces. He interrupts himself to answer the telephone. When he has a discussion with a visitor, he grabs a white marker to make points on a blackboard.

After the Matamoros murders, Ponce-Rojas met with Francisco Blanquet, one of his top investigators.

Blanquet, short, dark, muscular, had come to talk to the boss about the ugly business in Matamoros and the man, Constanzo, that police everywhere were looking for.

"He's here in Mexico," Blanquet said. "I am sure of it."

The "Mexico" Blanquet spoke of was what most Americans call Mexico City. For the foreigner in Mexico City it can be confusing to discover that there is no such place. Mexicans refer to their capital simply as Mexico. There is the Republic of Mexico, and the State of Mexico, which surrounds the capital, but technically, legally, there is no such place as Mexico City. Officially it is known as the Federal District, and by all accounts it is the heart of the largest metropolitan center on earth, with perhaps twenty million inhabitants. What we call Mexico City is a city of neighborhoods, known as *colonias,* and of *delegaciones,* which could be compared to the boroughs in New York.

Constanzo here? Ponce-Rojas thought. "Why do you say that?"

"The Zumpango River," Blanquet said. "Claudia. It is the same. Bodies being carved up."

Ponce-Rojas nodded. Perhaps Blanquet was right.

215

Through the window of his office Ponce-Rojas looked down at the tree-shaded plaza that fronted his own building and the borough hall, next door. It was lovely, he thought. He wanted his building to be inviting to the public and had in fact already begun renovations. We must win back the confidence of the citizens, he thought, and we won't get that looking like a jailhouse. From his window he could also see signs of the less lovely Mexico. A stray dog ambled about the plaza, and in the parking lot urchins hustled drivers for change.

"The Zumpango," Blanquet repeated.

"Yes, the Zumpango," Ponce-Rojas said, bringing his thoughts back to more somber matters. "And Claudia."

The cases, Blanquet was suggesting, bore the fingerprints of Adolfo Constanzo.

"They were before my time," Ponce-Rojas said. He had only been on the job since the beginning of 1989.

Ponce-Rojas, who had previously had a very successful private practice, had taken the job of regional attorney reluctantly, out of a sense of public duty. He did not really want the job because law enforcers in Mexico have a very bad reputation, and it's been getting worse. In Mexico City there is a common perception that the police force of 25,000 teeters always on the brink of anarchy. The low point for the world's most populous city had come the previous September when two police forces had collided. Armed members of the Federal District Police had stormed the Mexico City headquarters of the Judicial Police to free two fellow officers who were being held for assault and robbery. (Roughly the equivalent of the Washington, D.C., police attacking FBI headquarters.) In one subsequent newspaper poll, 76 percent of the people in Mexico City said they had no confidence in the police department.

But Ponce-Rojas took the job because the man who appointed him was one of Ponce-Rojas's former teachers and had told him, he says, that "I had a duty to take this job. We are engaged in a war—a war on crime—and in wartime your duty is to serve your country."

Though Ponce-Rojas had not been in office during the Zumpango and Claudia cases, he knew what Blanquet was talking about.

"Our people had been looking for this bunch since 1987," Ponce-Rojas says. "That year the police discovered the remains of six persons who apparently had been ritually murdered in a factory on Calle Barcelona. This was long before I assumed this present position, but from what I've been told, occult paraphernalia was found at the site, mystic symbols smeared on the walls in blood, that sort of thing.

"The bodies were butchered, cut up in pieces by someone who knew what he was doing; parts of the remains, hands and feet tied together, were tossed in garbage bags and dumped in the Zumpango River.

"Businessmen in Mexico sometimes call in a priest to bless a new enterprise," Ponce-Rojas says. "But these people planned to make money distributing cocaine in fire extinguishers. They called in a satanic group to conduct a black mass complete with human sacrifices.

"A year later we had a similar murder of a homosexual, someone they called La Claudia at Calle Londres thirty-one."

Calle Londres, or London Street, is on the edge of the Zona Rosa, the pink zone. After the discovery of the dismembered bodies in the river, a team of a dozen detectives spread throughout the area, talking to dealers in amulets and potions, but they found out little.

"The magic generally is pretty harmless stuff," Ponce-Rojas says. "At times an animal may be sacrificed, but not people."

The investigators did hear about a house that had been used for black masses and satanic rituals, but by the time they got to it everybody who had allegedly been involved was gone. The investigation stalled out.

But then in April came the murders in Matamoros. Blanquet, who had led the Zumpango investigation, was convinced that there was a connection between those murders and the Matamoros massacre.

"I want to reopen the investigation," he said that day in the office.

"Okay," Ponce-Rojas told him. "We'll do it. This time we have names. We know who we're looking for."

After the April 17 raid on Constanzo's house, Ponce-Rojas came up with the name of Salvador Montes (either from Teresa Quintana, or from Benitez in Matamoros). Montes, an alleged member of Constanzo's gang, was arrested on April 24 and charged with the murder of Claudia. Montes claimed that the killing had been done by Constanzo, who sacrificed the victim as part of a satanic rite.

"Where can we find Constanzo?" they asked.

"Colonia Cuauhtemoc," Montes said.

That neighborhood, named for Mexico's last Aztec ruler, lies to the north of Reforma Boulevard, the main avenue in the capital. In the forties the area was fashionable. Now it is a bit seedy, the sidewalks are cracked, and the plaster is chipping from the facades of the four- and five-storied apartment houses along its tree-lined streets. The area, near the American and British embassies and several of the better hotels, is now a popular nesting spot for foreigners.

"We start checking around and we find this supermarket," Ponce-Rojas says. "There they tell us about a young woman who tried to pay for her groceries with a hundred-dollar bill, and the store didn't want to take it. We have a lot of trouble with counterfeit dollars in Mexico. Anyway, this girl said the store could trust her, that if there was any trouble with the money she lived right across the street at Calle Río Seña nineteen."

The girl fit the description of Sara Aldrete. It was a good lead but the investigation had to be stalled. Teachers had been on strike in Mexico and the labor unrest was threatening to turn violent, so Ponce-Rojas had to keep his men available in case of trouble.

On Saturday, May 6, the alert ended and Blanquet requested permission to take his men back to Colonia Cuauhtemoc. Ponce-Rojas agreed.

"We spotted what looked like the Chrysler New Yorker which we understood Constanzo owned, and we were checking it out when all hell broke loose," Blanquet says. "Bullets and fifty-dollar bills were falling into the street. For a second we didn't know what was going on. People were running out after the money like they didn't think the bullets could hurt them. There was a woman talking on a street corner pay phone paying no attention to what was going on. One of us had to drag her away. She must have thought she was being mugged. There was another woman in a wheelchair who got up and ran away. Never came back for her wheelchair, either."

Blanquet's story has to compete for credibility with several others. According to the official version put out by the procurator's press office, detectives were inspecting what appeared to be an abandoned car and suddenly found themselves under fire. Also, early press releases put out by the police department just after the shootout suggest that the police had no idea they were battling the notorious Constanzo cult.

In still another version of events, Sara Aldrete says the police knew where the gang was because she tossed a note out the window when she saw police in the area.

Neighbors, however, say that the police arrived after some of them called the police to complain about shouting and gunshots in the apartment. One woman who lives in the same building says she heard a loud argument and a woman's voice saying, "Kill him," followed by six shots. All of this, she says, happened before the police arrived. Pedro Solis, a juice vendor whose stand was shot up during the gunfight, says, "It was a loud argument. They were saying vulgar things. I'm sure someone called the police."

We can get another perspective on this incident from the words of Alvaro de Leon, El Duby, who was in the apartment on Río Seña, along with Constanzo, Omar Orea, and Martin Quintana.

"I was sleeping," El Duby said the following day at a press conference. "Constanzo woke me up. He was like crazy, shouting it was all over, throwing money and gold coins out the window and shooting. He grabbed a batch of money and threw it out the window, and then he began shooting, not paying any attention to where, and shouting that everything was lost. He kept shooting all the time. It was Sara who first saw the detectives prowling around outside. She told Constanzo and that was the end of everything."

Though Blanquet's men were in plainclothes and unmarked cars, they suspect now that the antennas on the trunks of the cars gave them away.

Blanquet's boss, Federico Ponce-Rojas, recalls being in his office that Saturday at noon.

"It had been a rough week and I was thinking about knocking off early when the emergency call came over the radio. I grabbed my gun and we were off."

The firefight on Río Seña lasted for forty-five minutes. By the time it was over, eighty plainclothesmen and a hundred uniformed cops were on the scene. Miraculously, nobody was killed. One police officer, Carlos Padilla-Torres, was wounded. "But they bandaged him up and he was back in line before it was all over," Ponce-Rojas says.

According to Blanquet, Constanzo was the only one in the fourth-floor apartment shooting. "He was raking the street with an Uzi," Blanquet says. "Two others stood by and handed him fresh magazines. Our idea was to keep him shooting until he ran out of ammunition. We wanted to take him alive."

After the shooting stopped, Blanquet's men stormed the building.

But Constanzo was not to be taken alive.

Here, according to El Duby, is what happened inside the apartment:

"All I heard is shouts of 'They're coming.' Adolfo went crazy and started to scream that they would kill him and that we shouldn't hide. He told me to kill him and Martin. I told him I couldn't do it, but he hit me in the face and he threatened me that everything would go bad for me in hell. Then he hugged Martin Quintana and I just stood in front of them and shot them with a machine gun."

Specifically, Constanzo and Martin, who had been "married" in what Aldrete said was a "voodoo ceremony," walked into a closet, sat down, and closed the door. Constanzo ordered El Duby to shoot him. El Duby squeezed the trigger of his machine gun and a hail of bullets crashed through the door and ended the life of Adolfo Constanzo and his lover.

222

Sara Aldrete, who was also in the apartment, backs up El Duby's story.

"El Padrino ordered him [El Duby] to kill him because it was the end and he wanted to die with Martin," she says.

When Blanquet and his men got into the apartment, they found the bloodied bodies of Constanzo and Quintana in the closet. With guns drawn they made their way up to the roof of the building where they found Sara Aldrete, El Duby, and Omar Francisco Orea Ochoa. The gang members, out of ammunition, were easily captured.

Another version of this story would later be issued by Mexican authorities, who charged that Sara Aldrete gave the order for El Duby to shoot Constanzo, and that all of the gang members had agreed to a suicide pact, but that police broke into the apartment before they could carry it out. The discrepancy in stories would become part of the continuing mystery of Sara.

When police went through the apartment, they found black, red, and white candles, black robes, two swords, a plastic skull, a rattlesnake's rattle, dolls, and other religious items. They also found partially burnt money. Constanzo's followers told them that El Padrino didn't want anybody else to have the money.

"Sara was a terrible housekeeper," says Ponce-Rojas. "We found the apartment in a shambles when we got in there, and not just because of the shooting. It looked like nobody ever washed a dish or threw anything out. They had empty wine bottles and beer bottles sitting around. And pieces of roast chicken that must have been days old were still sitting on the table."

Later they arrested Maria del Rocio Cuevas Guerra, the forty-three-year-old former model who had done some cult recruiting for Constanzo in Mexico City. Ponce-Rojas says that Guerra acted as an agent for the gang and had arranged for the rental of the Río Seña apartment. A press release later issued by the city attorney general's office said that she had been found in a house that had been converted into a temple for the worship of Satan.

Police questioned the suspects all night long. According to Ponce-Rojas, El Duby told them he had avoided being caught up to now because he had been blessed during a black mass. He said that he had met Constanzo when he took part in a voodoo ritual at the ranch. During that rite, he said, he had sacrificed a human being, stabbing him with a knife. The body, he said, was buried near the ranch. (This body, apparently, has not been recovered, unless El Duby meant that it had been buried on the ranch.) Ponce-Rojas says El Duby also confessed to taking part in the murder of Mark Kilroy. When the murders were discovered, El Duby said he went first to McAllen, then to Las Alamedas in the state of Mexico, then to Cocoyoc in the state of Morelos, then to an apartment on Calle Jalapa in Mexico City, and finally to the apartment on Río Seña, where he killed Constanzo and Quintana.

Later, when he was asked to describe Mark Kilroy's behavior just before the cult sacrificed him, El Duby said, "He was very quiet."

Maria Guerra told police she helped Constanzo

only because she was afraid of what he might do to her children.

"I was having a run of bad luck," she later told a reporter. "So I went to him. He made some marks on my back and killed some chickens."

A spokesman for the attorney general's office later told the press that Guerra "made a business out of black magic." He said that the ten suitcases taken from her house were all filled with black magic paraphernalia.

During the all-night interrogation Ponce-Rojas found Sara Aldrete to be the most fascinating member of the group, and he considers her to be the most "wickedly depraved."

"We questioned her for fourteen hours," he says, "and she was unfazed, and obscene. Cesar [Gomez, the prosecuting attorney] is really *mocho* [extremely religious] and he was very uncomfortable. You might have thought it was the devil herself."

On May 7 the newly captured cult members were trotted out for the press, just as their comrades in Matamoros had been. This time the suspects were placed behind a table on which police had placed burning candles, swords, black robes, and wax skulls that they had found in the apartment after the shootout.

El Duby was the first prisoner to be brought out. The lights flashed, the cameras whirled, and the reporters shouted.

Question: Why did you join the sect?

Answer: Because I had a problem in Matamoros. I had killed a person there, and in the ritual I met some of the people in the sect who could help me.

Q: How did it happen?

A: Well, we went into this little temple, a little house, and we stood around and we saw the *padrino* place a body in a cauldron.

Q: Why was that done?

A: Because Adolfo said it would go better for us in the future. He said that we would receive protection, but Adolfo was the only one who committed the murders after someone else kidnapped the victim.

Q: How long had you been in Mexico City?

A: I came here about eight months ago because of the crime I committed in Matamoros, and I really don't know about most of the things they done since I really joined the sect because they offered me protection. Constanzo and I came to Mexico because when we were in a hotel in Brownsville, we were told Elio was arrested and it would be better if we went to Mexico City.

Q: How were you initiated into the cult?

A: I joined and got this blessing so I would have better protection, and they marked me, but I don't know just what they did because I was blindfolded.

Q: What is the difference between other types of religions and what your sect practices?

A: I don't know anything about religion, but I joined the sect because the father of the person I killed in Matamoros wanted to kill me.

Q: What was the relationship between Martin and Constanzo?

A: Martin was his right-hand man.

The next person to speak was Omar Francisco Orea, who was identified by the attorney general's office as a twenty-three-year-old student at the National University of Mexico. Orea had been living on Calle Havre in the pink zone, about ten blocks from Río Seña 19.

Q: How long did you know Constanzo?

A: I met him six years ago when he came to Mexico for the first time.

Q: What rituals did you participate in?

A: Only those in Mexico City, none of the ones in Matamoros. They never sacrificed anyone here, but I know the sect was involved in the deaths of eighteen people. Last July 17 Constanzo killed a homosexual called Edgar something or sometimes Claudia. He cut him up and put the pieces in plastic bags he carried away in a gray Lincoln. [This murder, of course, did take place in Mexico City. Apparently, Orea is saying that nobody was sacrificed during rituals at Constanzo's house in Mexico City.]

Q: Where did all those dollars come from?

A: The money was the result of his activities in narcotics trafficking. He said something about robbing banks, too, but I don't know which ones.

Then it was Sara Aldrete's turn to speak. Wearing a purple T-shirt under a brown leather jacket, she was trembling noticeably when she spoke.

Q: Supposedly your participation in these rituals was to protect you from arrest by the police. How do you feel now about your participation in those rituals?

A: I don't believe in any of that. I am in the religion Santeria Cristiana [Christian Santeria]. Adolfo initiated me last year. I was still learning

227

about it and he was showing me all these things, and he gave me some saints that I had in my house, Saint Francis, Saint Barbara, the Virgin of Charity, and the Holy Child and some others. I really am very confused about all this. The other part of my religion is Palo Mayombe. I didn't love Adolfo, but I followed him. I feel terrible about all that has happened.

Q: Do you think that with your arrest the sect is finished?

A: No, I don't think it is over with us because there are many people in this religion. The things that they found in my house had nothing to do with satanic rituals. They were saints, just as I have said.

Q: Who killed the victims?

A: Jesús Adolfo Constanzo.

Q: Where else outside of Matamoros and Mexico City were these rituals carried out?

A: I don't know anything about that, and the sect was just us and the others who have fled. Only in these places.

Q: How did you choose the victims for your sacrifices?

A: When all of this came out on television, I couldn't believe it. It was amazing. I asked the *padrino* how all this had happened, and he said this was done by the people in Matamoros.

Q: After every sacrifice did you eat the human flesh?

A: I was never present, but as far as I know, nobody did that. They only deposited the remains in a receptacle.

Sara also said that she wanted to apologize to the family of Mark Kilroy.

"I feel sorry because when he disappeared I was trying to help the [Kilroy] family." (Though she did not elaborate at the press conference, Sara later claimed that she had helped by putting up posters of Mark around Matamoros.)

When asked how she got involved in the cult, she said, "I don't know how I got involved. It was like knowing everything was one thing, and then having it be something else. If I had known it was like this, I wouldn't have gotten in it."

Apartment 14 at Río Seña 19 is sealed now. The five-story building looks like any other, unscarred except for the broken windows on the corner of the fourth floor. A plumber has his shop next door, and beyond that there is a business specializing in children's parties. There is a video rental shop around the corner along with a coffee shop. Across the street there is a nice restaurant. On May 6, employees and customers at all of these establishments were herded into back rooms when the shooting started.

"We never really knew what was going on until we saw it on television that night," says Felix Valdez, who lives across the street. "All I can say is that landlords should be more careful who they rent to. But they say Constanzo had more money than God and he probably paid a big deposit. These days you can't argue with that."

TEN

The Aftermath

On May 7, police said that the two bloody corpses found in the closet at Río Seña 19 had not positively been identified as Constanzo and Quintana. There was speculation that Constanzo may have feigned his own and Quintana's death, and that the two had escaped. (According to one published report, a woman who lived in the building claimed to have seen two people escape.)

Armando Ramirez of the U.S. Drug Enforcement Administration in Brownsville said, "We wouldn't put it past them to kill two other people and substitute the bodies. They're shot up pretty bad. I think there's a twist to this thing."

Later Mexican police confirmed that Constanzo's and Quintana's bodies had indeed positively been identified by fingerprints, and that Quintana's brother also identified the body. Constanzo's body had fourteen bullets in it. Quintana's had nineteen.

Also, on May 7, Gertrudis Jimenez, next-door neighbor to the Aldretes, told Sulilpsa Luque of the

Brownsville Herald that Sara Aldrete "was a normal girl and there was never anything unusual about her."

Jimenez said she had known Sara ever since "Sara was a pretty five-year-old girl who used to play with my children." Jimenez said that she was still "between believing and not believing" what she had heard about Sara. "We saw her friends and Constanzo a few times," she said. "He was always well dressed." She said Sara had lots of friends visit her in her upstairs apartment, but "we never heard parties or anything and there was never much noise."

On May 8, Oran Neck and George Gavito visited with Sara Aldrete. When the men returned and talked to reporters, Gavito expressed disappointment that Constanzo was dead.

"We wanted him alive to find out what ticked him off to do that stuff," Gavito said. Of Sara, he said, "She would talk to us like a witch. She was being rude. She never cried. She was cold. Cold."

Oran Neck was widely quoted as saying that Sara had a "split personality," which led to speculation that Sara had a multiple personality, like "Sybil." Neck, however, was not speaking quite so literally.

"Sara has kind of lost touch with reality. No question about it," Neck said. "Her dual personality is coming up pretty strong right now. When you talk to her without the TV cameras there, she's pretty truthful.

"It seems like when the cameras come on, she kind of reverts back to this nice, young, clean-cut kid from Texas Southmost College."

George Gavito adds, "When the cameras were there, she was real nice. When she was with us, she was the same ol' witch."

On May 9, Mexican police arrested, but did not name, another alleged member of the Constanzo cult. The attorney general's office also announced that Sara Aldrete had implicated Adolfo Constanzo's mother in the group's voodoo practices. Sara, allegedly, claimed that El Padrino's mother knew everything about the group's activities in Mexico.

On May 10, Juan Benitez told the *Brownsville Herald* that there was little chance that the cult members in Mexico City would come to Matamoros for trial, since there had been homicides in Mexico City.

"But it is not the end for us," Benitez said. "We still need Ovidio Hernandez and Mario Fabio Ponce."

Benitez told a reporter that the cult was a "circle of homosexuals."

"Sara was only bait to lure men to the sect," he said, "but on the other side all are homosexual." After reiterating what was known about the cult, Benitez added, "There is no way we could have made all of this up."

On May 17, Sara Aldrete told the *Houston Post* that after she was taken into custody, eight officers blindfolded her and tortured her for most of the night. She said she was given electric shocks, was beaten, and nearly suffocated. She said she was also "almost raped." She said that when she was taken to the district attorney's office, she was told by agents, "We are going to do to you all those things that your beloved Constanzo did to others."

Later, when George Gavito was asked about the torture on the TV show "The Reporters," he replied, "If she was tortured, that was probably one of the best things that ever happened to her. I don't think she was tortured."

On May 23, a Miami judge set $2,500 bond for Adolfo Constanzo's mother and set August 15 as the hearing date for her to appeal her sentence of two years for stealing a refrigerator.

On Friday, June 19, Elio Hernandez said at a hearing that his confession had been tortured out of him by Federal Judicial Police. He said that the months in jail have been "okay," but that when he and the others were in police custody, "We were tortured real bad. We had broken ribs."

Elio and his friends were being kept together in a cell where they spent most of their time watching a thirteen-inch, black-and-white television. "They are in good condition," says one guard. One woman who works at the prison says the men get two hot meals a day. "Sometimes they eat better than we do," she says.

As for the charge of torture, Juan Benitez says, "I have never arrested a man who has not claimed when in jail to have been tortured."

On May 20, the body of Adolfo Constanzo was sent home to Miami. Constanzo's brother Fausto said that funeral details would not be released. He did not want the press or public intruding into the family's grief, he said.

"This is going to be a very emotional time for us," he said.

On May 26, Texas attorney general Jim Mattox awarded certificates of appreciation to Oran Neck, George Gavito, and Juan Benitez.

On July 16, Lisa Baker, writing in the *Brownsville Herald,* revealed that U.S. drug investigators had tied the Matamoros cult into a vast drug network that spread all across the hemisphere.

"By comparing notes on narcotics suspects in the Rio Grande Valley, various federal agents established a pattern of drug trafficking from the Hernandez family in Matamoros to top Chicago mob bosses," Baker wrote. She said that law officers believe the Hernandezes and their cohorts "comprise one leg of a giant smuggling organization," and added that "in-depth investigation of the Hernandez family's ties to organized crime began at least as early as August 20, 1988."

July 17, in an interview published in the *New York Times,* Jim Kilroy said, "Who do we blame for our son's death? We blame people like ourselves who let this [drug use] go on."

The Kilroys, who were trying to get five million signatures on a petition for a federal crackdown on drugs, had formed an antidrug organization called M.A.R.K. (Make A Responsible Kommitment).

"If we couldn't put our energies into this," Helen Kilroy said, "it would be a much more difficult time for us."

ELEVEN

Sara

When I began this book, I knew that some of the questions I had about the case will never be answered. The acts of Adolfo Constanzo and his followers were kept secret not just because they were against the law but also because they were woven into the fabric of a secret African religion. Furthermore, mass murderers such as Adolfo Constanzo tend to take their secrets to their own graves.

But to me the greatest mystery to emerge from the events in Matamoros and Mexico City is not buried in a shallow grave. It resides in the mind of Sara Aldrete.

Who, exactly, is this young woman? Is she a friendly college student who somehow got caught up in something bigger than herself? Or is she some truly demented person whose evil we can hardly even imagine?

I began asking about Sara Aldrete on April 25,

two weeks after she, Adolfo Constanzo, and others had dropped out of sight. At Porter High School on International Boulevard in Brownsville, I met with a teacher who had taught Sara during her sophomore year. The teacher looked up and down the long school corridor to make sure no one was watching us. Then she opened the door of a small supply closet and turned on a light.

"In here," she said to me. "We can talk in here."

We went into the closet. The teacher closed the windowless door.

"Yes, I remember Sara," she said of the girl who was in her class at age fifteen, nine years ago. "She was a very friendly girl. Very friendly." "Friendly" is the word I would hear again and again about Sara. "Everybody liked Sara. She was a tall girl, skinny, with a baby face and curly hair."

"Smart?" I asked.

"Yes, very smart. Her grades were excellent. And she was very polite. I liked her a lot."

There was a worried look on the English teacher's face. She was wringing her hands. She was actually trembling. What on earth was she going to tell me? I wondered.

"I only had her for that year. Some of the Mexican kids from Matamoros will do that, transfer over to here for sophomore year."

"What else?"

"Huh?"

"What else do you remember about her?"

"That's it," the teacher said. "She was an ordinary girl so I don't remember much about her."

"No weird jewelry, no Satanism?"

"Goodness, no. She was a good kid, a real good kid."

I glanced at the closet door, which had been locked. "But why all the secrecy?"

The teacher's eyes widened. "Don't you know what those people *did?*" she said. "They have not caught all of them. They could be anywhere. I don't want them to know I talked to you."

"I see."

The teacher opened the door. She poked her head out, looked around. "It's okay to go now," she said.

As I was leaving she called to me, "You're not going to use my name, for sure?"

"For sure," I said.

Later the same day, on the campus of Texas Southmost College in downtown Brownsville, I sat on a stone bench with Jack Loff. It was a hot afternoon and the deep-blue Texas sky was almost cloudless. The campus of this two-year college is small and friendly. Low and modern buildings blend in eye-pleasing ways with the Spanish-colonial architecture of the older buildings. From where we sat we could hear the *wop-wop* of tennis balls being hit back and forth by Sara's classmates on the courts where Sara sometimes played. In the distance we could hear the sound of students, playing baseball, or shouting out their weekend plans. Now and then students walked by and said hello to Mr. Loff.

Jack Loff is the volleyball coach at TSC and head of the physical education department, where Sara worked afternoons as a secretary. He is a tall, bearded man, thin and athletic. He leaned back on the bench and lowered his arms under him for support as he stretched his long legs.

"Sara?" he said. "I guess most of all I would say that she was friendly. Very, very friendly. When she came to work in the afternoon, she would say hello to everybody. When she left at night, she would say good-bye to everybody. One time she went on vacation with her parents, and when she came back, she brought presents for everyone. She brought baseball caps for me and one of the other fellows. She got something else for the ladies. Very thoughtful."

"Athletic?" I asked.

"She was a great fan," Loff said. "A tremendous supporter of the teams, always active. She was the driving force behind the soccer boosters club. But she was not very good with sports. It seems she wanted to be a physical education teacher, and she always seemed serious about it and sincere. But she didn't know how to do things in sports. It was as if she had never played anything."

"Do you think she's dead?" I asked.

By this time police all over North America were looking for Sara and Constanzo, and there were rumors that Constanzo had murdered her.

"God, I hope not," Loff said. "I don't believe she did all those things. I certainly don't believe she's any kind of godmother. I think Sara just got caught up in something. You know, you get involved in one murder, and that forces you to go along with the second. I think after the first murder it's a case of, you participate in the next murder or you'll be the next victim.

"I mean, think about it. If you were really some sort of godmother, if you really thought you were a high priestess or something, it would start to show in the way you dressed, in your jewelry. You'd start to talk about it. I never saw any sign of that with Sara. I always thought of her as superstitious, but not overly so, just in the way that is typical of that culture."

Loff stopped. He stared down into his hands. It seemed he had done some thinking about this. "She was an ordinary girl," he said, perhaps struck by the strange fact that he was discussing a young woman who, in the short time since her disappearance, had become a subject of great fascination to people all over the world.

"You know," he said, "talking about this religion and all, it seems as if kids these days don't have anything important to believe in. It used to be they had the Vietnam war, but now there is nothing for them to latch on to."

After that Loff didn't speak for a while and it seemed that the silence was saying that the conversation was over. Loff, it seemed, had little more to say about Sara Aldrete than did the teacher at Porter High School. I waited. Sometimes people need time to remember, and then to decide what to tell. So far Loff had not said anything that he didn't tell the reporters, dozens of whom had swooped down on Brownsville and Matamoros when the bodies were found. Virtually everybody who was interviewed about Sara said "nice," "friendly," "pretty," and "kind."

"You know," Jack Loff finally said, "Sara took volleyball and sailing under me, and I never once saw her in a pair of shorts. I remember thinking, gee, she wears sweats every single day."

"And?"

"I don't know. It's just there were some odd things about her, things I haven't mentioned to the media."

"Like?"

"Well, the week before all this happened, I think it was Monday, Sara called in and said she wouldn't be in to school for a couple of days, and she wouldn't be in to work. She said she was in the hospital, she had been in an automobile accident. And then she came to school the next day, she was all bandaged up, and she had her neck in a sling and bandages across her chest. Well, she had done this before. She would call in and say she wasn't coming to school, and she'd have these weird, weird stories, about some drunk beating her up or something. One time she said she'd had an accident and some guys had gotten out of the car and beaten her up. Another time she said there was a dog barking outside her house, and when she had gone out to check on it, there was a guy there and he beat her up. Weird stories like that. This was all in the past nine months or so.

"So when she called in that Monday, I just blew it off as another one of Sara's fairy tales. Then I heard from the kids that Sara said her car was totaled out, and some of the guys who play basketball said, 'Hey, her car ain't totaled out, she drove it to school today.' Weird. Then the following week, on the Thursday before the bodies were found, Sara showed up and said good-bye to everyone. She was leaving school, said she had some kind of physical problem or something, and wanted to say good-bye to everybody because she might not be back. After the bodies were found it was obvious to me that Sara must have known they were getting close.

"She didn't seem frantic or anything, it wasn't like she was in a rush to get out of there. We were sad to see her go, but we were all glad she had come by to say good-bye."

Jack Loff, like many of the students, was troubled by the knowledge that TSC was perhaps best known as the college that Sara Aldrete and Serafin Hernandez went to, and by the fact that their notoriety might interfere with his one chance to make the school famous for something else.

"Damn near won the national volleyball championship last year," he said. "Took the team to the finals in Miami. Finished second. But I tell you, this Sara publicity is going to make recruiting for next year hell. Already lost one girl. Big girl, five ten, good player. Had her all set to play next year, then this happened and her mother yanked her out. It's a shame. What Sara did had nothing to do with the school. She could have been going to school anywhere."

If Jack Loff's memories of Sara Aldrete seem ambiguous, he is not alone. Sara is a woman of mystery and of contradictions. She led, it seems, two lives. By day she was the all-American college girl in Brownsville. She was an honor student, the soccer booster who is listed in "Who's Who in American Junior Colleges." By night, it seems, she lived across the border in the bizarre and deadly world of drug smugglers and ritual murderers. Though Sara's degree of involvement with the murders has yet to be established, certainly Sara had some role in the cult of Adolfo Constanzo. It was this "Jekyll and Hyde" aspect of Sara that captured the headlines and the imagination of the public after the bodies were recovered and the fugitives were identified.

Sara's worlds were not completely sealed off from each other, and certainly with each trip across the International Bridge she scattered about some clues to her dual existence. But there was never anything to suggest a connection to mass murder, and only after she was gone would the people who knew Sara at Texas Southmost College begin to dredge their memories and say, yes, now I see it.

Sara was often seen on campus with her young Cuban friend, Constanzo, but it seems that he was not an alarming figure to students. He was just some guy whom Sara knew, and the people who do remember him seem to remember mostly that he drove a fancy car.

But Sara's own car was certainly a cause for suspicion, and it had set a few tongues awagging even before she disappeared.

About six months before the discovery at Santa Elena, Sara started driving to school in a new red 1988 Ford Taurus. Police later learned that she had paid $12,000 cash for it.

"Suddenly, she just had this new car," an acquaintance from the college says. "Brand-new. And she was from a poor family. In fact, she was on scholarship and she wasn't making much money. How could she suddenly afford such a nice car? And the car had a telephone in it. We asked her, Sara, what do you need a telephone in your car for? She just shrugged and said a friend gave it to her."

A few days after Sara began appearing in the newspaper as a "witch," a "godmother," and a "madrina," several students who knew her gathered in the presence of *Brownsville Herald* reporter Rebecca Thatcher and talked about their classmate, with the understanding that their names would not be used.

One young man said he had always thought it odd that a young woman with a $3.35-an-hour work-study job could have a cellular phone with monthly bills that, Sara had told him, were as high as $250 or $300.

The young man also said, and the other students agreed with him, that Sara wore unusual necklaces and warned people not to touch them, because something bad would happen.

"She would wear these medallions and she wouldn't let anybody touch them," he said.

Other students recalled that Sara liked to wear black.

At the time there was also a rumor that Sara had tried to recruit male TSC students into the cult. Guy Garcia would later describe it this way in *Rolling Stone* (June 29, 1989):

"[There is] . . . a story making the rounds that

tells of the night Aldrete persuaded three male friends to screen a video of *The Believers*. After the film, say the students, Aldrete stood up and began to preach in strange tones about the occult. 'They had been drinking and they just thought she was trying to be spooky,' says one student who knows the boys, 'but they look back at it now and think she must have been serious.'"

If the hint of witchcraft and bloody murder was not enough to make Sara a star, there was also a good measure of sex thrown in.

In Brownsville no one seemed to think Sara had a wild sex life.

"I remember her talking about guys," Jack Loff says. "She would mention this guy or that one and say she really thought he was cute or she liked him, real girl stuff, and I'd see her with a guy from time to time, but that's all."

However, reports from Mexico portray Sara as quite the hot number.

When Elio Hernandez was questioned by Juan Benitez, he told the commandant that he was introduced to the cult by Sara Aldrete, with whom, he said, he was having an affair. He said that at age fourteen he and Sara were *novios* (a relationship that implies everything from being sweethearts to being engaged), and that after Sara got divorced they began going out again. He claimed that Sara was the godmother of the cult, and he went on to praise her bedroom technique, especially when it came to oral sex.

At the Matamoros press conference, Serafin Hernandez Garcia said that he, too, had had sexual relations with Sara. "She was the best. Incredible. I never felt anything like it," he said.

Police in Texas alleged that Sara used sex as the bait to lure one cult victim into the hands of his kidnappers. Later, from Mexico City, there would be more reports that put Sara in bed with Adolfo Constanzo and Omar Orea Ochoa.

On Tuesday, April 11, the day the bodies were being dug up, eight federales went to the home of Sara Aldrete's parents at 86 Santos Degollado in Matamoros. There they learned that Sara lived in an upstairs apartment that had been added on to the small cinder-block building a year earlier. "We never go in there, that is her property," Israel Aldrete, Sara's father, told police.

Inside the apartment police found black candles, beaded necklaces, and cigars, all near a blood-stained altar.

"The candles were on the floor in a circle," says Sara's father. "That was what formed the altar."

Sara's family was shocked. They had never seen the items, they said. They knew Sara to be a sweet, helpful, kind, and thoughtful Catholic girl, they said. They could not believe this, they said.

Though Sara's family decided to avoid the press, Robert Kahn, a reporter for the *Brownsville Herald,* did get to speak to Sara's father.

"I just got lucky," Kahn says. "I happened to go over there when he came out to close the wrought-iron gate in front of the house."

Señor Aldrete's eyes filled with tears and his voice trembled as he talked to Kahn.

"Sara tried to help the entire world," he told the reporter. "She loved children, she loved animals, she loved the beggars who needed money. We never saw anything bad in her. We don't believe that she did a thing like this. It's very hard, painful. All the neighborhood knew her as a happy girl. She always behaved well. She was an excellent student, with many scholarships, many diplomas. She was very content and happy. No one can believe it. It's like we're blindfolded."

Kahn is certain that Sara's parents knew nothing about her cult activities. "I believed her father," he says. "The man was crying. It was obvious that he was in shock over the whole thing."

As the days of April passed and May began without any new clues as to the whereabouts of the fugitive cult members, the mystery of Sara Aldrete grew. More and more Israel Aldrete, and the rest of Sara's family, along with a mesmerized public, wondered if they would ever get to hear Sara's side of the story.

After Sara Aldrete was arrested and put in jail, she did have a few brief opportunities to speak to the press before Mexican prison authorities put a three-month moratorium on her access to journalists.

She said that she didn't know anything about the murders, that when she found out about them she became scared. She said that she tried to leave the cult, but they wouldn't let her because they were afraid that she would turn them in. (There could be something to this. One of the other women allegedly in the cult has said that she was afraid for Sara's life one day when Sara went off in a car with Constanzo and Quintana.)

Sara said that there are friends of the Godfather who are on the loose and might still harm her.

She said that she had sexual relations with several members of the cult, including Adolfo, who sometimes introduced her as his wife. "I had fun with a few of them," she said. "Omar was the last." (In fact, it has been reported that she was "sharing kisses" with Omar when the police arrived.)

She said she never took part in the rituals, that she was only at the ranch once, for a birthday party. (Domingo Reyes has said he saw her there several times, and some cult members have said that Sara participated in the rituals. El Duby, however, has backed up Sara's story that she was not involved.)

Sara described life on the run. From the airport in Mexico City, she said, they went to a house on Jalapa Street. They spent most of their time in an apartment there, watching television, not going out. They moved around. They slept in cabins for several days, then went to the apartment where they were caught. "My life was hell," she said. "I never knew when they might kill me. It was horrible." She said that Constanzo said he would kill her parents if she tried to run.

She said she misses her parents.

She said that she's been tortured by Mexican police and prison officials.

In June, 1989, Sara wrote to me and said she wanted to talk to me "about all those things that I don't even want to mention on this piece of paper."

Sara is being held at the Reclusorio Oriente, the

Eastern Detention Center in the Federal District. It is, as the name implies, on the eastern edge of the capital district. To get there you drive out Tlahuac Avenue past small factories, warehouses, and distributors of plumbing supplies, then turn down a street of cinder-block houses and stores. From a distance the Reclusorio might be taken for a large high school or community college. It is spread out over what might be two city blocks with large concrete plazas bordered by green shrubbery and lawns.

Mexican trials are made up of several hearings, often over a period of a year. At each hearing written evidence can be presented by the prosecution or the defense, and witnesses can be called. Sometimes the prosecution and defense counselors simply square off against each other, presenting their conflicting statements, with the judge acting as mediator.

On July 19, 1989, in Juzgado 58, there was to be another hearing in the Sara Aldrete trial. (A *juzgado* is a courtroom, and it is from that Spanish word that we get the English word, "hoosegow.") Located at the Reclusorio Oriente, Juzgado 58 doesn't look like a courtroom. It could be any bureaucratic office. A white Formica counter separates an area of desks and chrome and plastic chairs. The manual typewriters on top of the desks are not old, but they are worn out from wear. Two policemen wearing bulletproof vests cradle their automatic weapons carelessly. They are the sort of cops you might see outside any bank in Mexico City. On the far wall of the courtroom there is a grilled window. From the other side of the grill the prisoner witnesses the proceedings, the taking of depositions and the presentation of evidence. There is no bench, no bar, no jury box, no gallery for spectators. A visitor can wander about at will.

Behind the grill on this particular day was Sara Aldrete. Sara, at six one, is remarkably tall for a Mexican. She has hazel eyes, an olive complexion, and dark hair. She is attractive, but far from beautiful or even what one might call pretty. Except for her height, Sara looks like a typical Mexican college girl and she appears younger than she is. Just a few weeks shy of her twenty-fifth birthday, she leaves the impression that by the time she is thirty she will probably be fat. On this particular day she comes across as sweet, vulnerable, certainly not the "witch" that Gavito and Neck saw.

While the Mexican authorities have told me that I cannot visit Sara in jail, this *juzgado* is a public place, and because some of the expected witnesses have not shown up, there is time for Sara to answer the questions I have prepared.

Sara, who was with her lawyer and her father, was not surprised that permission to speak with her had been denied.

"Ponce won't let anybody talk to me unless they pay him first," she said. "It is a good thing that he is not here today. He charged a television crew two thousand dollars and told them that I needed the money to pay for my defense. I do, but I never saw a penny of it.

"First they made a scapegoat out of me, and now I am being exploited."

For a moment, it seemed that Sara was going to cry.

Sara had been held in solitary confinement since her arrest. She lived in a cell that was perhaps five feet by ten and contained no furniture. She ate on the floor, she slept on the floor.

"I was the one who told them where Constanzo was," she said. "I threw a note out the window from the apartment on Río Seña nineteen. My lawyer has it. [Sara's attorney confirmed that the note has been filed as an exhibit for the defense.] A woman picked up the note and stopped a patrol car. Now the police say they were investigating what they thought to be a stolen automobile, but that's a lie. This woman showed them my note. Adolfo had kidnapped me and threatened to kill me. I wanted the police to come."

The remainder of the interview with Sara Aldrete on July 19 went as follows:

Question: How did you get involved with the cult?

Answer: Everything they say about me, everything you read about me, it's a lie. I only knew Constanzo a little more than a year, and then he wasn't in Matamoros all the time. He didn't live there.

Q: What about Elio and Serafin? The things they are saying about you?

A: The federales told them what to tell the press and that's what they did. You don't know what it is to be tortured. They let you go and you don't want to be tortured again, so you say whatever they want you to. . . .

People don't know that I am a vegetarian, that I am opposed to killing animals. They don't know that I belonged to the animal defense league, that the one thing I could never accept about the Santeria Cristiana is that you are supposed to sacrifice roosters.

Q: How did you learn about Santeria Cristiana?

A: Alfonso taught me. [She calls Adolfo "Alfonso."] And I was fascinated by it. It is a religion that does not interfere with your being a Catholic, only the difference is that you can worship the saints in your home. Build your own altar. You leave little bits of fruits for offerings, but Alfonso also said you had to sacrifice a rooster and I could not go along with that.

It is a very old religion that has its origins in Africa and has been practiced in Mexico since the seventeenth century. It is very strong in Veracruz.

Q: What about the accusations that you smuggled marijuana into the United States, and drove a new Ford which you had paid for in cash?

A: Alfonso gave me that car. He said he was in love with me. I was not in love with him, but he had bought the car and registered it in my name, so I said I would accept it if he would let me pay him for it. He never would, so I gave the money to Martin, some every month.

Q: Did you know about the murders? Did you know they were sacrificing people at the ranch?

A: No. No. Alfonso was at the Brownsville Holiday Inn and I went and confronted him, asked him what it was all about, and he confessed to everything. Then he said I would have to stay with

251

him now that I knew everything. If I escaped, he said, he would go after my family, my parents, my sisters.

Q: Did you have chances to get away?

A: Yes. Alfonso decided we should fly from McAllen, Texas, to Mexico City. He thought no one would expect us to travel in that direction. But I didn't have the right documents. I had no passport, only a card identifying me as a Mexican citizen entitled to live in the United States. So the others left, and I had to wait for the next flight while the authorities were issuing me another visa.

I followed Constanzo to Mexico City because I was afraid and I had no one else to turn to. I was afraid for myself and I was afraid for my family. Once I rejoined them, I was even more afraid.

Alfonso kept saying that he was going to kill me, poison me, or shoot me. One day he put the barrel of a machine gun in my mouth and asked his little voodoo dolls if he should pull the trigger. He claimed they told him no, that I was too tall, too big to fit in a garbage bag, so he let me live. All I wanted was for somebody to save me. And now I'm here.

Maybe I am better off in jail. Everybody thinks I'm such a monster.

After Sara was taken away to sign documents, her lawyer, Victor Fernando Perez-Salas, remained to answer more questions.

At thirty-seven, Perez-Salas has been practicing law for fifteen years. Slight of build, he is a partner in the law firm known as Grupo Jurico Satelite.

(Ciudad Satelite is a prosperous suburb north of Mexico City.) Standing in a courtroom, waiting for a hearing to begin, he is happy to explain the Mexican legal process, as it applies to his client.

A suspect, he says, is brought in for questioning and may be held for seventy-two hours. "Although," he says, "there is not much he can do if he is held longer." The suspect, also referred to as the accused, has a right to have an attorney present, but he can waive that right or have a public defender assigned to him. The accused is asked to make a statement or declaration of guilt or innocence, which he will then sign. In most cases, Perez-Salas says, the statement amounts to a confession, and he claims that these confessions are usually obtained through torture.

"Squirting soda water up the nose or holding a suspect's head in a latrine bucket," he says, are allegedly favorite methods "because they leave no bruises."

"Torture, of course, is illegal," he adds, "but difficult to prove."

Perez-Salas explains that once the statement is signed, the accused may be presented to the press for questioning, as were the cultists in Matamoros and in Mexico City. Later the signed statement, containing either a clause waiving the right to have an attorney present or the signature of a public defender, is presented during arraignment proceedings. He says that repudiation of a confession is normally not accepted.

"The logic," he says, "is that either the suspect

was lying when he confessed or he is lying when he claims the confession is not valid. One way or another, he is a liar. So he is held without bail."

In some cases, such as Sara's, the confession is minimal, but a magistrate will rule that there is sufficient evidence to hold a suspect and proceed with a trial. The trial is conducted by a criminal court judge, without a jury. Most of the evidence will be presented in written briefs. There are question-and-answer sessions that are open to the public. The prisoner watches the proceedings from behind bars in a cell adjoining the courtroom.

In the Federal District (Mexico City), Sara Aldrete is on trial for murder, criminal association, and obstruction of justice. She has confessed to accompanying individuals she knew to be fugitives from justice, failing to notify the authorities, and being present at the murder of Constanzo and Quintana.

Sara has also been indicted for violating federal health statutes related to narcotics smuggling.

In Matamoros, Sara faces more charges.

Perez-Salas says he will try to prove that Sara was kidnapped by the fugitive cult members and that she stayed with them out of fear for her life. He has presented in evidence a note that Sara claims to have thrown from the window of the Río Seña apartment and that, she says, led the police to the hideout. Perez-Salas says that this is proof that Sara was held against her will.

Perez-Salas says he will go on to show that Sara has no criminal record and has never been in trouble with the law, that she was, in fact, a model citizen.

"I will not plead insanity," he says. "Sara is not mad."

Outside the Reclusorio Oriente, Israel Aldrete, Sara's father, lingered for a few minutes to talk.

Israel Aldrete has iron-gray hair that has turned white at the temples. His white mustache tends toward yellow. He is six feet tall, slender. On July 19, he wore a dark-brown leisure suit and looked very much the provincial in the big city. At sixty-seven he is retired as a clerk with the Mexican Federal Electricity Commission.

"Don't believe all these things they are saying about Sara," he said. He spoke only in Spanish. "They are not true. Everybody who knows her knows that she is innocent. She is the best daughter that a man ever had." His voice was quiet, melancholy. Israel is the father of three daughters. Sara, almost twenty-five, is the oldest. The youngest would soon turn twenty.

"She never gave us a moment's worry," he went on. "She was always home early in the evening, usually eight-thirty or nine, almost never later than ten. When she would go to those conferences the college sent her to in Houston or Dallas, she would call us the moment she arrived to let us know where she was staying and that everything was all right.

"She had two scholarships at Texas Southmost College," he said. "She was studying for her master's degree. They gave her one to help with tuition, the other to help with her living expenses. They accuse her of smuggling marijuana and say she had all that money. I'd like to know where it is. We had to accept help from friends to pay for her defense and we still don't have enough."

Israel Aldrete and his wife were staying with friends in Mexico City while their daughter was on trial.

"They questioned my other daughter, too," he said. "Did terrible things to her. She refuses to tell me what. The authorities in Mexico are animals."

For a moment he stared back at the prison walls that separated him from his daughter.

"The failure of her marriage," he said. "That was a great disappointment. It made me very sad. We have always been good Catholics."

"Why did the marriage fail?"

Israel shook his head. "I don't know. Sara never wanted to talk about that. Maybe she told her mother, but not me." He smiled slightly. "Maybe she thought I'd go after her husband. But I am not like that. We are not violent people."

Senor Aldrete, looking much older, perhaps, than he did four months earlier, did not speculate on the future.

"All I know," he said, "and I know it in my heart, is that Sara is innocent. She is a good girl."